This book by Renee Berry reveals  very tough and challenging time can relate to as Renee pours out her heart ... M000086864 for being completely transparent helping others to find comfort and encouragement in your struggles and the comfort you found in God's Word. Thank you for the wonderful scriptures you shared from the Amplified Bible bringing us to know and understand God's heart for those who suffer. His presence with you even when you felt so far away is truth to which we all can cling in life's most painful moments.

—CINDY WEST
Serving Christ with Ethnos360
Author of *Living in Christ Our Source of Peace*

Renée has been delivered from "the pit" and "the shadow of death!" She is not advocating that we wait until a major crisis comes to allow Jesus to restore our soul. No, Berry encourages us to hear Jesus ask us to invite Him to deal with every skewed thought, painful emotion or devastating choice in our "inner man." We are to do so now and every day of our lives.

—CLARENCE LEDFORD
President, Life Discipleship International

As a long-time survivor of Stage IV cancer, I can highly recommend this book to people dealing with cancer or any trial. Renée transparently reveals the internal turmoil which comes with being diagnosed with and fighting cancer. She shares how Jesus gently navigated her through the maze of lies and confusion of pain and doubt. As a strong proponent of the New Covenant Jesus instituted, I so enjoy her emphasis on all that He has given us: a new heart; a new spirit; and His Holy Spirit as well (Ezekiel 36). She glories in her inheritance in Christ in the face of pain, an example we all can follow!

—JOE FORNEAR
Director, Stronghold Ministry

To Lovey,

July 2018

INVITE HIM IN

Jesus in Seasons of Adversity

RENÉE H. BERRY

with JOY!

Rée

HIGH BRIDGE BOOKS
HOUSTON

DEDICATION

To those who seek intimacy with Jesus Christ amidst difficult circumstances, relationships, trials and tribulations. I especially pay tribute to Julie Beasley, my editor, who during the most difficult year of her life, worked tirelessly and sacrificially with me to make this manuscript what it is.

CONTENTS

PREFACE

Each entry is written to be directed either to you, the reader, or to highlight a conversation between The Lord Jesus and me. My hope is that this style will draw you in to partake of my journey while better grasping His unyielding, everlasting, pursuing love for each of us.

May I clarify that this book is not written just for cancer patients. It is written to declare that Jesus Christ really is Enough amidst any adverse part of life's journey. Trials and the temptation to believe otherwise come through trauma, a long, long illness or a loss that requires a season of grief. How do you stay afloat mentally, emotionally and spiritually when all systems seem to be failing or when you reach up out of the pit uncertain if anyone is going to be there to pull you out? Any trial comes complete with grief, that myriad of emotions that "feel" so real! What do you do when all of your inner resources seem to be spent?

As you are looking for answers amidst the trial and grief, do not be alarmed to find that we all have cancer. Physically, there is the potential for normal good cells to develop mutations that lead to cancer. Just as devastating is the fact that we are subject to cancer of the soul (mind, will and emotions). When we believe lies about God, self and others, these deceptions eat away at our soul. We must intimately connect to and depend on Jesus every minute of every day in order to believe Who He is and Who He says we are (John 6:28-29). He is the only Truth. He is the only cure! The world, our own flesh and the devil are constantly on our heels to render us ineffective in the Kingdom of God.

I have been remarkably, miraculously healed of Stage 4 Hodgkin's Lymphoma—dangerously close to death with a tumor coming through my chest wall. The following pages contain excerpts from my journal. It is like no other story because it is mine alone. How astounding that nobody's journey is the same. Why did He heal me? Deuteronomy 29:29a is the answer to that! "The secret things belong unto the The Lord our God." No one can answer why I was saved but not my precious friend's husband. He was diagnosed at the same time I was and has gone to be with Jesus. I remain to give an account of my journey with cancer of the body and soul and the horrendous grief process that was a part of that journey. My prayer is when trauma hits you, and I am sorry but in this world it will, this story will impart to you the answer to your dilemma. It lies in Christ alone. He is Enough and longs to be that for you. **Invite Him In.**

> Psalms 40:1-5 - I waited patiently for the LORD; And He inclined to me and heard my cry. He brought me up out of the pit of destruction, out of the miry clay, And He set my feet upon a rock making my footsteps firm. He put a new song in my mouth, a song of praise to our God; many will see and fear and will trust in the LORD. How blessed is the man who has made the LORD his trust, and has not turned to the proud, nor to those who lapse into falsehood. Many, O LORD my God, are the wonders which You have done, And Your thoughts toward us; There is none to compare with You. If I would declare and speak of them, they would be too numerous to count. (NASB)

Author's Note

We hear God speak to us primarily through the revealed, written (*logos*) Word, the Holy Bible, God's inerrant Word. Because He is one with us, Spirit to spirit, we also hear Him in our minds and hearts. Over and over in these writings, I encourage you to go to The Lord Jesus and exchange your feelings and the lies that battle your mind for ownership; the very thoughts that keep you chained and in bondage to your feelings. Jesus died to make this possible. (Galatians 5:1)

The *rhema* (spoken) word is God's whisper of intimacy to you.

> John 10:3 – The watchman opens the door for this man, and the sheep listen to his voice and heed it; and he calls his own sheep by name and brings (leads) them out.

He desires that intimate relationship with you so He can minister to you personally. No one really knows how you feel except Jesus. He will never speak intimately to you in contradiction to the Scriptures. That is why I bid you to **Invite Him In.** Whether He speaks to you through the Scriptures, His *logos* Word, or He whispers to your heart, His *rhema* Word, He offers a personal relationship. The invitation to be intimately involved with Jesus was made 2000 years ago because of the finished work of the cross and still stands today. **Invite Him In!**

ACKNOWLEDGEMENTS

I pen this with fear and trembling that someone will be left out! Thank you seems like such a trite phrase. Sincerely, from the bottom of my heart, **THANK YOU** to the following who made my journey bearable.

My Mother – Thank you for being my forever prayer warrior who interceded for me. At the age of 96 you took a taxi to come to the hospital after an emergency emission to check on your "chick"! I love you! You are amazing! I am sorry you could not stay with us to see the book finished. God called you Home and after 99 years, seven months and six days, you said "Goodbye" to us and "Hello" to so many loved ones waiting on you with Jesus! Yay Mama! I know you will be cheering me on!

My daughter, Jennifer – Thank you for dropping your life to come to me. You are a wife, a mom, a teacher, a praise team leader. You said, "Mama, I'm not waiting another month, I'm making arrangements to come now!" And come you did, unselfishly trying to meet my every need. You became my nursemaid, cook, housekeeper, encourager, medical assistant, chauffeur, personal attendee—no holds barred; you were willing to do it all. I will never be able to express my heart of gratitude to you. I hope you know what is in my heart for you—unconditional love. You are the only one who knows for sure that my socks talk under the influence of hydrocodone and morphine!!!

Joel Paul Blackburn, Jr - my son-in-love, affectionately RD - Thank you for delighting my daughter (and me) by flying with the girlies to visit. Thank you for letting your life and household be interrupted by me for three long months. Hey, you would not have become the gourmet chef that you are had Jen not been away! My question is have you cooked anything since she got back??? I love you boy!

My son, Keith, and daughter-in-love, Andrea - Thank you for being willing to be called upon. I am grateful for your help with my care and doctor's visits. Keith, remember when they pulled out the three-foot long PICC line? Your eyes got so big and you sat straight up in your chair! I am grateful to you both for the groceries, meals, repairs around the house and lifting groceries out of the car. I was able to buy them; I just couldn't bring them into the house! Andrea, I love our theme song "Overcome". I can never stand by you and sing it without tears! My loves, I am grateful for your continued ministry to and love for me.

Beth, my niece, my nurse – Thank you for your concern and compassion as you came and changed bandages and drained the chest tube—all those yucky things. You brought me the gift of your fun personality and laughter every time. No words can express my heart so please know I am forever grateful! Thank you, Allen, for giving up your wife all those hours!

Josie, my personal medic - Thank you for the blood pressure and heart rate checks, PICC line maintenance, groceries and groceries and more groceries! Not just any groceries, but the best from Whole Foods! Wow! What a gal! I love you!

Marie, my niece – Thank you for being involved in this all-too familiar-journey; one that you took with your precious Mama. Thank you for encouraging Jennifer. WOW, I loved all the salmon! You continue to be the bomb, baby! I love my times with you.

My PICC line "nurses", Keith, Chris, LeeAnna Renée and Kyle Lee - Thank you for making the best team day in and day out for nine long months!

LeeAnna Renée – Thank you for Your constant ministry to me by spending time online figuring out what would be the best natural remedies to kick cancer (remember the wheat grass?). Your research was precious to me. I always smile especially when I think about your seat on the end of the sofa by my chair which was close enough for you to reach over and rub my arm. I believe your pure love helped to heal me. There are no words to express my love for you.

Annika Grace, my precious sugar bear - Thank you for being the first one to lay your hand on the chest tumor and pray it away! When the news did come that there was no more cancer and no more tumors the first year after the chemo ended, you knowingly said, "Yeah, Jesus told me that when I prayed for you the first time!" My tea and water glasses were always full! Your love completely consumes me. I am a better person knowing you! Love you!

Kyle Lee - Thank you for those healing times when we played board games. Your precious words, "Mimi, I didn't know what I would do if my Monopoly buddy wasn't here!" soothed my soul. Your Monopoly buddy lives! Thanks for rescuing me by lifting all the heavy stuff for me. You have such a servant heart. I love you more than words!

Little Maddie, big Maddie now, you'll always be my baby grand girl - Thank you asking the big question, "Mimi are you well enough now for Mimi camp cause Mimi camp rules?" Music to my ears! I'm so glad that we have been able to go again and make some more memories! You are deeply loved princess angel!

Dalton, my special boy - Thank you for coming to visit. You ran to me with great concern when you heard what was going on. You asked the question that haunted us all, "Mimi, you are not going anywhere, are you?" No, God chose for me to stay. I am still right here! You are a heart string to me. I love you!

My Healing Team: Claudia, Debbie, Denyse, Ellen, Fran, Gayle, Jerry, Linda, Maria, Melba, Michelle, Nancy, Pat G., Sandy, Sharmane, Sherri, and Vicki - Thank you for being my precious sisters and brother my friends who walked more than the second mile with me. You stood with me by taking me to chemo treatments and Doctor's visits, bringing meals, buying my groceries, taking me shopping, taking me out to eat, housekeeping chores, staying with me, phoning me—prayer warriors all. It takes a village to get someone through chemo treatment! Thank you for taking time out of your lives to make mine better. I will never forget your sacrifice. I love you all!

Jaye and Mary Dale and the Grace Haven family, my Jesus family - I appreciate the daily visits, phone calls, communion, and prayer, prayer, prayer. You are a true picture of Christ's love. I am eternally grateful!

My family at Grace Life International - Thank you for your continued love and prayer support. I will never know the number of prayers until God starts turning the prayer bowls of heaven over! I love you all! You make me well!

My Grace Life International Support Team and Project Hope Support Team – Thank you for your gifts and prayers. They are an eternal investment. May God richly bless you for your many sacrifices, time in prayer and financial support.

Prayer warriors across the world – Thank you! You delivered me from the brink of death and so many days of depression and feelings of despair into the lap of Jesus as you stormed heaven! There I found rest for my weary soul and healing to remain on this earth! I told somebody one day that there are so many people praying for me all around the world that God probably was tired of hearing my name and said, "Okay! Okay! Here's the plan. She's going to live!" Thank you for standing in the gap!

*The Many—you were referred to in one devotional as those who came to pray, anoint, encourage and lay hands on me personally - Mark and The GLI Freedom Fighters, Pastor Jaye and Mary Dale, the elders and their wives of Grace Haven Church, Pastor Bob and Ellen, Pastors Todd and Julie, Karen, Jen, LeeAnna and Anni, Pastor BJ and The Bridge Praise Team and the five hour girls, Tammy and Tracey (how about ten hour girls when you had to turn around and go right back to Tennessee and greet a newborn grandchild that decided to come that night!). You are all true heavenly gifts!

Dr. Martin Herbkersman and James Courtney, Naturopath - Thank you for being one with me in understanding the paths I chose for my well-being. Knowing you both brought health and wellness!

Dr. Steve Madden, Paula Cox NP, and the team at Lexington Oncology – Thank you for your fervent prayers! Yes, Dr. Madden, I truly am a miracle!

Oh! Chemo brain is for real! I hope I have not left anyone out. If I have, you are loved and appreciated! Thank you!

INTRODUCTION

The doctor stood before me shaking her hands, visibly manifesting her confusion. She said, "This is serious! It's leaking!" I asked, "What's leaking?" She replied, "I do not know! It's just leaking. I am going to make you an appointment with an Oncologist. I'll be back in a minute." With that, I was welcomed into the world of cancer! **Let me back up 33 years**.

In my late twenties and early thirties, I was diagnosed with rheumatoid arthritis. I remember standing before my unopened window in the hospital, there for ten days of grueling tests, and I was unable to open the curtains because of the weakness in my hands. As I am a degreed musician and keyboard player and made my living with my hands, I was devastated. I could not get up and down without tremendous pain; I could not lift my precious babies; I could not play my beautiful piano. I was faced with the decision to begin to take various medications, mostly for pain, have my joints injected with gold or seek another route. Unfortunately, I could tell that I was already dependent on the medication. It turned me into a walking zombie who screamed and yelled at my children. I hated it and my reaction to it. Besides, it did not take me out of pain; therefore, I took more than what was prescribed—not a good thing! I was also told my hands and feet would become terribly deformed and I could always have reconstructive surgery. I told the Lord at that point if that was what He wanted, I would face it, but if not, I was willing to go another way. I believe He showed me His Way. I began to clean up my diet—that meant no more Pepsi and Heavenly Hash ice cream floats every night (you think?)! Yes, sweets were my nemesis! I began to gradually incorporate whole foods and over the years refined that to what I liked and could tolerate. I was always deemed a "health nut". Little did most people know the pain I would suffer from "just one or two" brownies or cookies or "just one bowl" of ice cream. Surely that "little bit" would not hurt! I beg to differ when your immune system is so compromised that your body is in constant pain. It does not take much to start the flame that burns and radiates through the joints and connective tissue. At first, I was so lawful with my family, insisting they eat what I eat. Over the years, I have learned how wrong that was. There is a right and wrong way to impart a healthier life style to others than how I did it, but that's another story for another time. I also began to be very serious about learning what alternative medicine and therapy would offer me.

Fast forward 30 years… I noticed a lump on the right upper chest one morning. It seemed to just appear. I had extensive blood work that indicated an elevated level of lymphocytes, thought to be stemming from a strep infection. After treatment, I did not feel unwell, so I continued my quest to live well—eating unprocessed foods and exercising and being healthy and free of pain. As I have gotten older, I have considered my life style as preventative. I planned to enjoy my latter years pain free, with no arthritis, no heart disease and certainly, no cancer! I began to lose weight with no adjustment to diet or exercise. I had carried an extra 10-15 pounds since menopause and I was delighted to be shed of it! I began to see Dr. Martin Herbkersman, Doctor of Chinese Medicine and Acupuncture in Columbia, SC. He did not like the looks of the lump on the chest. He immediately sent me to a primary care physician who x-rayed and then scanned me—thus, the Doctor's shaking of her hands and the ensuing Oncology appointment. There was nothing leaking. What the doctor saw on the CT scan was one of two large masses on the right lung surrounded by an unusual amount of fluid.

With the experience of 30 years of Naturopathic medicine that served me well (through rheumatoid arthritis and hepatitis from contaminated seafood, neither of which do I blood test for now), I believed that I would also tackle cancer with a Naturopathic protocol. However, I wanted to consider all my options, so I took the Oncology appointment. Unbelievably, I had been at peace with what was happening. I will admit the peace was laced with denial and pride, at times. "How can this be? I have taken such good care of myself. Surely, this is not the stage IV lung cancer or Lymphoma that the scan suggests!" My experience of watching others take chemo and observing the devastating side effects did not lead me to want to jump on that bandwagon.

My initial visit with the Oncologist was my very first encounter with cancer treatment. Until then, I had been very upbeat. In the waiting room, I witnessed downcast faces, bald heads and people using oxygen. This was the first time that fear gripped me. I cried out, "Lord!" and immediately heard in my mind, "Psalm 41". I quickly turned to the passage which was downloaded on my phone and read it in the Amplified version. Here are the first four verses,

> Blessed (happy, fortunate, to be envied) is he who considers the weak *and* the poor; the Lord will deliver him in the time of evil *and* trouble. The Lord will protect him and keep him alive; he shall be called blessed in the land; and You will not deliver him to the will of

his enemies. The Lord will sustain, refresh, *and* strengthen him on his bed of languishing; all his bed You [O Lord] will turn, change, *and* transform in his illness. I said, Lord, be merciful *and* gracious to me; heal my inner self, for I have sinned against You.

I began to personalize the passage, replacing the "him" with "I" and "me" and reread it. I sat stunned and immobilized. I am very grateful they did not call me to see the doctor right away because I was frozen. I was able, during the consultation, to mention this to my doctor, a man of faith. I asked him what was I supposed to do with such a dramatic speaking of the Lord? He replied, "Hold onto it, Sister!" And hold onto it I have!

I desired to avoid traditional chemicals in my body. My Oncologist supported me with the promise that he would check my blood levels and conduct the necessary scans to monitor my progress or lack thereof. In the beginning of treatment, I chose an alternative protocol designed by a Naturopath who had conferred with medical and naturopathic doctors in California. I looked well, felt very well and continued living my life—teaching, traveling, being a Mama to my kids, and a Mimi to my grands. I was confident that the Lord was in the process of healing me. I never thought it would be instant. The passage of Scripture (Psalm 41) seemed to indicate a transformation—a process of sorts. Five months later, I suddenly began to deteriorate. It was evident that the disease was getting ahead of the treatment. My weight took a dramatic drop; suddenly, my heart rate skyrocketed when I would move around. This did not resemble healing to me. I wish I could tell you I held on and turned to the Lord at every turn, but I often succumbed to my feelings of despair and believed the lie God was untrustworthy. It is not that I did not believe He could heal me. In my mind, it was, "Would He heal me?" Psalm 41 said He would! My question became, "I believe You. You spoke to me, now where are You?" I knew He would never leave me or forsake me, but I planned a funeral! Therefore, it did not feel as if God was going to move on my behalf in this world. I knew the Truth that He is Eternal Life (I John 5:20) and I was going to be fine, whatever happened. I surrendered to going Home but wondered about the promises in Psalm 41. I believed He meant healing for NOW, not in heaven!

It was time for my Oncology appointment. As I weighed in at only 118 pounds the decision was made to begin chemo after six months on the alternative protocol. My doctor promised me he would not let me suffer. I was very certain that this would be my demise. After a week in the hospital and numerous, very painful procedures, I was prepped for this regimen. I had to wait for two more months while the doctors were researching what type of Lymphoma it was. I lost six more pounds! The diagnosis of Hodgkin's Lymphoma finally came after I had a lymphotomy and within a few days, I had my first chemotherapy. I was wheeled into a private room hooked-up on oxygen weighing 112 pounds. The impending question was would my heart survive the first treatment? Praise God! Since that day I have experienced improved health despite the side effects from chemotherapy that are still present with me today.

What was my spiritual condition? Let me framework this by saying I know Jesus took my shame to the cross. However, I felt ashamed of my temper tantrums. I hated my distance from God. I also knew it was up to Him to restore me. I would wait patiently (or not) for Him to be the Lifter of My Head. The depression from the chemo was suffocating. When I was physically, mentally, and emotionally exhausted, I was not much good spiritually either. I knew the Truth. I had experienced, taught and counseled it. I was waiting and hoping for my feelings to line up so I would not feel so lost and alone. I felt very abandoned by the Lord, at times. All this was driven by lies and I knew it. My choice? Should I stand in the Truth (God is trustworthy), or should I give myself over to irrational feelings complete with lies. The battle was so intense that for weeks I just felt numb. I had chemo every two weeks. For the first week, I was relatively immobile. The second week my mind began to clear so I could emerge from outrageous feelings that had entrapped me just in time for another round. The vicious cycle continued for the duration of treatment. The after effects, natural or chemical, were devastating. The pain that was created was very similar to my rheumatoid days. The weakness was brutal. The cycle continued and, unfortunately, still continues today on some level as an after effect of the chemicals. I would often cry myself to sleep at night lamenting to God that I hated the way I felt about Him. I believed He was Who He says He is, but there was nothing in me that was feeling like He cared.

Do you remember the earlier passage recorded in Psalm 41? Not the healing passages, but the fourth verse,

> I said, "Lord, be merciful and gracious to me; heal my
> inner self, for I have sinned against You."

I could see He was transforming my bed of illness, but I had not taken this fourth verse into account. Since God's ways and even His thoughts are not ours (Isaiah 55:8), I began to realize in my foggy brain, that God wanted to heal my soul (renew my mind to Truth, comfort and heal my emotions and shape my will to His). He had definitely made me lie down in green pastures and led me beside quiet waters. (Psalm 23:2) Now it was His time to heal me. There was yet another layer in my soul that needed to be healed. His gift to us is to not let us remain in the lies that so affect our soul (mind, will and emotions) and our bodies. His desire is to make known to us, at a soul level, what He has already accomplished in our spirits—that which He accomplished on the cross, so that we could live free!

I knew what the deception was. "God, You are not trustworthy." I have a history, of which I am not proud, of judging God by my circumstances and feelings. God only asks us to do one thing—BELIEVE! (John 6:28-29) Believe Who Jesus says that God is and who He says we are. For the year I was in treatment, my God-given Word was "HOPE". I understood that if I placed my hope in Him, He would lead me where I needed to go—to the Truth of Who He is. What a journey! He is so Trustworthy and Faithful. That is His name; that is Who He is!

He then called me to "**INVITE HIM IN**". I encourage you to receive that invitation as well! **Invite Him In** to the pain, despair, hopelessness of your cancerous state—whether it be truly physical or that cancerous place in your soul (mind, will and emotions) that keeps eating away at the intimacy that God desires with you. I am sharing what Jesus is giving me about **Inviting Him In**. There is no "Life" without Him. These writings are for encouragement to those that have a physical, long-term disease (mine was cancer), unbearable grief from a loss or chronic pain; all grief sufferers and those who have cancer of the soul—a lie-based dis-ease of the mind that leads to unbelief and therefore, not experiencing Christ as Life (Colossians 2:10). I hope by **inviting Him in**, you will learn to be content in whatever circumstance you find yourself—a true Spiritual experience. By doing this, the circumstance may not change, but I guarantee, you will! **Invite Him In**!

1

JESUS IN THE PLAN

The current outcome for me is "successful treatment" and "remission." Backtrack with me to September 2012 when I was first diagnosed with Hodgkin's Lymphoma. Good health and vitality had come to a standstill. A few weeks away from what seemed like imminent death, I was experiencing what it would be like to leave this earth, even practically planning my funeral. Where was I emotionally, spiritually amidst this process? For many days I was angry, kicking and screaming like a two-year-old toddler until I learned to listen to His still, small voice calling, **"Invite Me In!"**

From the beginning, God gave me Psalm 41 (AMP). God, our Jehovah Rapha, chose to turn, change and transform all my bed of illness. This is still an ongoing process. As I have **Invited Him In,** I've found Him to be my Peace, Comfort and Stay on the long, long, long, same ole' days. You can **Invite Him In** as well.

> Psalms 41:3 - The Lord will sustain, refresh, and strengthen him (me) on his (my) bed of languishing; all his (my) bed You [O Lord] will turn, change, and transform in his (my) illness. (Parentheses mine)
>
> Exodus 15:26 - ...for I am the Lord Who heals you.

2

JESUS IN THE LOSS

Jesus, I find the quick mind You have blessed me with is fogged with drugs—drugs I can't even pronounce! I don't have the energy to even think. Yet, in the distant fog, in the stillness of a mind that cannot function, I hear that promised still, small voice. I need to listen.

You call to me whispering, "**Invite Me In** to every horror filled moment; every second of doubt and fear; every biting minute of pain; every ounce of chemo fluid that enters your veins. No matter what, because you believe Me, there is Life awaiting you. What you call life on earth or life in heaven can be experienced now. How can that be? I AM LIFE and I AM now—The Eternal Life. **Invite Me In!** What do you need Me to be in this moment? I AM your Everything and I hold all things together, especially you in this moment. **Invite Me In** to your every need, right now!"

I choose right now to **Invite You In.**

As I **Invite You In**, I find rivers of living water that refresh my soul.

> 1 John 5:20 - And we know that the Son of God has come, and he has given us understanding so that we can know the true God. And now we live in fellowship with the true God because we live in fellowship with his Son, Jesus Christ. He is the only true God, and he is eternal life. (NLT)

3

JESUS IN THE FEAR

I am learning from You there is sweetness in the possibility of facing my last breath. Sweetness? Yes, because the reality is and quickly becomes, it's just You and me, Jesus. Oh, there are loved ones with broken hearts and faces inches away from tears. There are also doctors, nurses and new friends that are in chemo to walk this journey. The friends and loved ones who earnestly, sincerely, faithfully run into the throne room of Grace and join with the Holy Spirit to intercede on my behalf, are present. Everything disappears when I place my head on the pillow for a nap or the night. Jesus, I hear You sweetly, intimately whisper, **"Invite Me In!"**

As I **Invite You** In, it is Your desire to remove my fears along with obstacles that hinder me from You like some giant Jericho wall. I know *obstacles* are simply feelings disguised as lies I am tempted to believe due to my circumstances. Truth will topple that wall! Time for the trumpets!

> Hebrews 11:30 - Because of faith the walls of Jericho fell down after they had been encompassed for seven days... (NASB)

4

JESUS IN THE QUESTIONS

Jesus, I **Invite You In** to this horror story I am living on earth; this terrible disease that has been unleashed. Why does an enemy exist who is allowed to torment me, cause me to decay so quickly in a cancerous state? My body may have cancer, or a long-term illness, or my heart might have a hole in it because of a loss, but I do not want to succumb to cancer of the soul (my mind, will and emotions)! I have pain and grief that attacks in hurricane style to seemingly wash me away. I am angry that this is what You, Lord, have allowed. Here I am face to face with You and I have a choice as to where to look. Do I desire answers to age old angry questions that even King David asked, or do I hunger for You in this moment? Do I desire understanding, or do I want to experience intimacy with You? I would so much rather be in Your lap than shaking an angry fist at You! I hear You gently, faithfully, lovingly whisper, **"Invite Me In!"**

As I choose to **Invite You In**, I find it's okay to be angry, even with You, Lord. You were big enough to handle it with King David; You are big enough to handle it with me. For today, I guess I've written my own Psalm 13! Now please get me to the, "But I have trusted...!"

> Psalm 13:1, 5 – How long will You forget me, O Lord? Forever? But I have trusted, leaned on, and been confident in Your mercy and loving-kindness...

5

JESUS IN THE GRIEF

Am I dying? Jesus rescue me! I have cancer—for what seems like an eternity I wait for results to start treatment. Hold on! Am I so entrenched in the world that, as a Believer in Jesus Christ, all I can see is my last breath here on earth, the sadness of leaving those and those things I love? Yes, grief is real—emotions are not to be denied. Therefore, I **Invite You In** so that in the process I can experience Christ's Life! I believe You will rescue me from this emotional pit! I know You long to exchange every emotion for a piece of Your Heart, Your Life, and make that real to me in this journey. I believe part of the experience of nearly dying here on earth is occurring to help me understand the Truth that You are Eternal Life. I **Invite You In!**

As I **Invite You In**, You whisper to my heart…

Job 42:5 - I had heard of You [only] by the hearing of the ear, but now my [spiritual] eye sees You.

Job 33:28 - [God] has redeemed my life from going down to the pit [of destruction], and my life shall see the light!

6

JESUS IN THE FEAR

Thank you, Jesus, for the strength to maintain much of my regular routine. I love the intimacy that allows me to trust You for many more days of endurance! I am blessed by the prayers and the love and concern of Your people. I pray for answers for financial security. I know You have all that figured out. I yield to You and I **Invite You In** to conquer my fears. What is the next step, Jesus?

As I **Invite You In**, I find when I release my fears to You, I begin experiencing the peaceful spirit of our union. I find You lighting my path.

> 2 Timothy 1:7 - For God did not give us a spirit of timidity (of cowardice, of craven and cringing and fawning fear), but [He has given us a spirit] of power and of love and of calm and well-balanced mind and discipline and self-control.

> Isaiah 61:3 - To grant [consolation and joy] to those who mourn in Zion--to give them an ornament (a garland or diadem) of beauty instead of ashes, the oil of joy instead of mourning, the garment [expressive] of praise instead of a heavy, burdened, and failing spirit--that they may be called oaks of righteousness [lofty, strong, and magnificent, distinguished for uprightness, justice, and right standing with God], the planting of the Lord, that He may be glorified.

7

JESUS IN THE SHOCK

What a year! I don't think I have words. This experience parallels a quote from the novel, *A Tale of Two Cities:* "It was the best of times; it was the worst of times."[1] A little context here might give clarity to my journey up to this point. I moved back to my home in South Carolina after living in Charlotte, NC for ten years and renting a home for a year in the mountains of North Carolina for work. It was wonderful to be reunited with family while living in my own home. At this point I received a hellish diagnosis—hurtful, overwhelming news book-ending the euphoric moments of renewed family gatherings. This was the deepest pain I ever felt. I walked the diagnosis, believing what Jesus spoke to me in Psalm 41. He told me He was going "... to sustain, refresh and strengthen me on my bed of languishing and turn, change and transform all my bed of illness." Just as He worked in King David's life, I believed He would "... not deliver me to the will of my enemies." I knew the enemy just wanted to kill and steal everything from me. His plan was to destroy me by rendering me ineffective. I did not have a clue how to walk this. I was so scared.

Jesus, I **Invite You In** to this horror story.

As I Invite You In, You remind me through Hebrews 13:8 that You are the same God of yesterday, today and forever. The same God Who spoke to King David.

8

JESUS IN THE GRIEF

I am fighting dreadful feelings of being unloved and uncared for by You, Jesus. In the grief process, I know the feelings are untrue, but I'm not denying them as they have continually washed over me—the disappointment, discouragement and loss of dreams I've had. This seems so damaging to my heart. I do not sit here as a victim, because I know You have filled the hole in my heart that no one else can with Your Life. Please come and minister to me as I exchange these feelings for what You want me to have today. I hear You whisper, **"Invite Me In."**

As I **Invite You In,** You impart to me the Word of Truth on which to focus. I can also experience You through other people whom You send to minister to me.

> 2 Corinthians 1:3,4 - Blessed be the God and Father of our Lord Jesus Christ, the Father of sympathy (pity and mercy) and the God [Who is the Source] of every comfort (consolation and encouragement), - Who comforts (consoles and encourages) us in every trouble (calamity and affliction), so that we may also be able to comfort (console and encourage) those who are in any kind of trouble or distress, with the comfort (consolation and encouragement) with which we ourselves are comforted (consoled and encouraged) by God.

9

JESUS IN THE WEAKNESS

Lord, I am grateful there is not much physical pain, just debilitating fatigue and weakness. My appetite is healthy, for which I am thankful. I am holding my own, waiting for the change that will take place when my body begins to receive nutrients and gain weight. I know that would be a sign of well-being. Also, seeing the tumor on my chest shrink would be so encouraging. I trust all that will come. I must **Invite You In** so I will not doubt what You have spoken to me in Psalm 41.

As I **Invite You In,** I find peace because You are Peace and You are present with me.

> Isaiah 9:6 - For to us a Child is born, to us a Son is given; and the government shall be upon His shoulder, and His name shall be called Wonderful Counselor, Mighty God, Everlasting Father [of Eternity], Prince of Peace.

> John 14:27 - Peace I leave with you; My [own] peace I now give and bequeath to you. Not as the world gives do I give to you. Do not let your hearts be troubled, neither let them be afraid. [Stop allowing yourselves to be agitated and disturbed; and do not permit yourselves to be fearful and intimidated and cowardly and unsettled.]

10

JESUS IN THE DOUBTS

These words of Truth run through my head this morning:

> Psalm 41:10-12 – Be merciful and gracious to me, and raise me up, that I may requite [avenge] them. By this I will know that you favor and delight in me, because my enemy does not triumph over me. As for me, You have held me in my integrity and set me in Your Presence forever…Blessed be the Lord.

I do not want to be a doubting Thomas, Jesus. Help me in my unbelief today. It is not a good day. I am simply too exhausted for anything except sitting here viewing the same scenery day after day. I have no energy to accomplish the simplest of things. I **Invite You In.** I totally depend on You to be my Strength.

As I **Invite You In**, I delight only in You and what You have imparted to me through Your Word, my thoughts and heart.

> Philippians 4:13 – I can do all things [which He has called me to do] through Him who strengthens and empowers me [to fulfill His purpose—I am self-sufficient in Christ's sufficiency; I am ready for anything and equal to anything through Him who infuses me with inner strength and confident peace.]

11

JESUS IN THE DISAPPOINTMENT

Thank you, Jesus, for the Peace which passes all my understanding. I am so grateful for the Joy that is manifesting and breaking through into my reality. It is my choice now to believe and live in the spirit. I am thankful You are here to walk with me through and carry me past this tremendous disappointment. There is an evil force which discourages me and desires to destroy me and render me ineffective. That is what the enemy wants. What do you want, Lord? I **Invite You In** to tell me. My Lord, please come rescue me.

As I **Invite You In**, I can experience You as my Peace and my Rescuer.

> Psalms 107:20 - He sends forth His word and heals them and rescues them from the pit and destruction.

> Philippians 4:7 - And God's peace [shall be yours, that tranquil state of a soul assured of its salvation through Christ, and so fearing nothing from God and being content with its earthly lot of whatever sort that is, that peace] which transcends all understanding shall garrison *and* mount guard over your hearts and minds in Christ Jesus.

12

JESUS IN THE DOUBTS

Pastor Joseph Prince states, "When you realize how much God loves you and you feed on His love for you, you will be supernaturally filled with the fullness of God."[1] I am thankful for this Truth.

I **Invite You In** to give my feelings to You, Lord. I desire to experience the Truth of Your love for me, even when I feel unloved. The major block in my believing You is the feelings that try to wedge between us like some jealous lover. Today, I choose to stand in Truth; my comfort is that I can substitute Your name for the word "love" in I Corinthians 13!

As I **Invite You In**, You reveal Yourself as Truth and Love.

> I Corinthians 13:4-7, 13 - Love (God) is patient and kind. Love (God) is not jealous or boastful or proud or rude. It (God) does not demand its (His) own way. It (He) is not irritable, and it (He) keeps no record of being wronged. It (He) does not rejoice about injustice but rejoices whenever the truth wins out. Love (God) never gives up, never loses faith, is always hopeful, and endures through every circumstance... Three things will last forever—faith, hope, and love (God)—and the greatest of these is love (God). (Parentheses mine)

13

JESUS IN THE PLAN

This was an incredible day, even though I felt rotten! My friend came over and we had a wonderful time and she came bearing gifts. Thank you, Jesus. Indeed, You are a loving Provider. Thank you for Your amazing embrace through my friends. I am overwhelmed with Your goodness. Thank you that I know the Truth of your love. My feelings have interfered. I trust You to rescue me and line up my emotions with Truth. I **Invite You In** to share with You!

As I **Invite You In**, I am thankful for Your goodness and faithfulness, Your willingness to minister to my broken, but grateful, heart.

> Lamentations 3:22-23 - It is because of the Lord's mercy and loving-kindness that we are not consumed, because His [tender] compassions fail not. They are new every morning; great and abundant is Your stability and faithfulness.
>
> Philippians 4:19 - And my God will liberally supply (fill to the full) your every need according to His riches in glory in Christ Jesus.
>
> Galatians 5:22 - But the fruit of the [Holy] Spirit [the work which His presence within accomplishes] is…goodness (benevolence), faithfulness…

14

JESUS IN THE DARKNESS

I wonder if friends know how important they are; how precious they are. They are so encouraging. I even feel much better emotionally around them! My feelings fluctuate, as if I'm on a teeter-totter some days. I am then catapulted into a dark emotional pit. Author Sarah Young reveals that Jesus gives a cause-and-effect explanation, "Share your hurts...I will soothe your pain. Share your joy...I will multiply it many times over. I am all you need."[1]

Sweet Lord, focusing on Truth and giving my feelings to You are the only life-giving avenues of escape from the pit! I **Invite You In** and pray that You will strengthen us all in our inner most being with Your Life and Love!

As I **Invite You In**, I can share with You, the One who really understands the suffering.

> Hebrews 2:18 - For because He Himself [in His humanity] has suffered in being tempted (tested and tried), He is able [immediately] to run to the cry of (assist, relieve) those who are being tempted and tested and tried [and who therefore are being exposed to suffering].

15

JESUS IN THE DISAPPOINTMENT

Last night, I had a nice visit with friends and dinner with family. I wish I could have pushed further and gone to the movies! I was just not up to it. After another night of chills and sweats, therefore, no rest, I'm too weak to go to church and am very disappointed.

I rest in You, Father. I **Invite You In** to the cell of this sick, sick prison. You are my Jehovah Rapha. Thank you for Romans 5:5, "God's love has been poured out in our hearts through the Holy Spirit Who has been given to us." That is the Truth and I am thankful, because when I ache so deeply, I tend not to feel loved. I **Invite You In** to remind me you have already filled that place. Nothing else can.

As I **Invite You In**, I am never disappointed with how You speak to me and minister to me in Your Word and by Your Spirit.

> Exodus 15:26c - ...for I, the LORD, am your healer. (Jehovah-Rapha)

> Romans 15:13 - Now may the God of hope fill you with all joy and peace in believing, so that you will abound in hope by the power of the Holy Spirit. (NASB)

> Ephesians 3:19 - ...and to know the love of Christ which surpasses knowledge that you may be filled up to all the fullness of God. (NASB)

16

JESUS IN THE DARKNESS

Thank You for the constant reminder that You love me, Jesus. I do not feel deeply loved at this moment. I'm discouraged about not feeling well while missing things I wanted to do this past weekend. I **Invite You In** so I can give everything to You. I know You are my All in All. Break forth, O Beauteous Heavenly Light. Shine in and through me as my Healer and Healing. I need you!

As I **Invite You In**, I am overcome with Light and Love.

> Ephesians 1:18 - By having the eyes of your heart flooded with light, so that you can know and understand the hope to which He has called you, and how rich is His glorious inheritance in the saints (His set-apart ones).

> Isaiah 9:2 - The people who walk in darkness will see a great light; those who live in a dark land, the light will shine on them.

> Isaiah 58:8 - Then shall your light break forth like the morning, and your healing (your restoration and the power of a new life) shall spring forth speedily; your righteousness (your rightness, your justice, and your right relationship with God) shall go before you [conducting you to peace and prosperity], and the glory of the Lord shall be your rear guard.

17

JESUS IN THE GRIEF

I arrived at my Doctor's office and during the appointment had a major breakdown while speaking to him. This uncontrollable display prompted something to awaken within me. After the dam broke, I experienced a myriad of emotions. I was surprised at the many, many tears which followed having been imprisoned by numbness for the past six months. Dr. Marty really ministered to me as he said, "Jesus, in His humanness, had his moments, too, and the profound thing is that He is here for us now to have our moments with Him." What an awesome Truth!

I am living out of my union with You, Jesus! Christ in me and me in Christ is the ultimate in **Inviting You In.**

As I **Invite You In,** I find that You invite me in to live out of my union with You!

> Galatians 2:20 - I have been crucified with Christ [in Him I have shared His crucifixion]; it is no longer I who live, but **Christ (the Messiah) lives in me**; and the life I now live in the body I live by faith in (by adherence to and reliance on and complete trust in) the Son of God, Who loved me and gave Himself up for me.

> Philippians 1:21 - For me to live is Christ [**His life in me**], and to die is gain [the gain of the glory of eternity].

18

JESUS IN THE SURRENDER

While lying on the table and receiving treatment at the Doctor's office, I cried out to You, Lord. I do not want to just resign to this part of my life's journey. That only brings anger, resentment, disappointment and discouragement. My eyes are focused only on my circumstances. I surrender to Your Love, will and plan. You promise You will work it for my good. I **Invite You In** to do just that. I yield to Your will being accomplished.

As I **Invite You In**, I am given up to believe by faith, not by sight.

> Romans 8:29 - We are assured *and* know that [God being a partner in their labor] all things work together *and* are [fitting into a plan] for good to *and* for those who love God and are called according to [His] design *and* purpose.

> 2 Corinthians 5:7 - For we walk by faith [we regulate our lives and conduct ourselves by our conviction or belief respecting man's relationship to God and divine things, with trust and holy fervor; thus we walk] not by sight or appearance.

> 2 Corinthians 5:7 - It's what we trust in but don't yet see that keeps us going. (MSG)

19

JESUS IN THE DECEPTION

What is keeping me from receiving Your love, Jesus? The answer was given in a moment of healing prayer, a vision, if you will:

> I could see myself standing with You in the garden watching as the serpent spoke to Eve. I heard You say, "I am good; I am love." I realized that, like Eve, I believed You withheld something from me. I repented of the lies and immediately, in my spirit eye, could see You pulling roots from my cancer-filled lung. You finally got to the bottom where there was a serpent, fangs wildly flaring. You took the serpent and flung it over the side of a cliff. You came running back and enfolded me in your garment, a cloak with a beautiful metallic sheen totally enveloping me. You opened my eyes to Your love.

All through the day I witnessed many ways You express love to me. I **Invite You In** to hold me securely and remind me when feelings seek to steal the Truth. I realize I have given territory over to the enemy for believing the lie that You are not trustworthy. I repent as I give You the deception that perpetuates my unbelief. Thank you for your forgiveness and the Truth that sets me free.

As I **Invite You In**, Your Light exposes the darkness (2 Corinthians 4:6). There, enveloped in Truth, I find freedom.

20

JESUS IN THE WEAKNESS

It is frightening to be unable to breathe because my lungs are filled with fluid. I don't feel strong today, but at least I find myself willing to stay put and rest. I trust this weakness is a result of this terrible illness and the treatment which ravishes my body. I do not see a change in my physical or mental well-being.

I dislike the circumstance, but I love You, Jesus! I **Invite You In.** My worth and acceptance are so tied up in doing and getting things done that I find Your thoughts on this lead me to rest. I believe You've got me covered!

As I **Invite You In**, I resolve, once again, to believe Your voice given to me and spoken through Your Word and Spirit. You never change.

> Psalms 16:8 - I have set the LORD continually before me; Because He is at my right hand, I will not be shaken. (NASB)

> Acts 17:25 - …nor is He served by human hands, as though He needed anything, since He Himself gives to all people life and breath and all things

> John 15:5 - I am the vine, you are the branches; he who abides in Me and I in him, he bears much fruit, for apart from Me you can do nothing.

21

JESUS IN THE DISCOURAGEMENT

Without believing the heinous lie that You, God, are withholding good from me, I have the freedom to grasp Your love today. I believe the following promise: You are not only going to keep me alive, but You are going to renew my strength like that of an eagle (Psalm 103:5). My hope is You. You are the fulfillment of that promise. I **Invite You In** to make that real in my experience.

As I **Invite You In**, You are there to encourage me to mount up and soar in You.

> Psalm 34:10 - The young lions lack food and suffer hunger, but they who seek (inquire of and require) the Lord [by right of their need and on the authority of His Word], none of them shall lack any beneficial thing.

> Isaiah 40:31 - But those who wait for the Lord [who expect, look for, and hope in Him] shall change *and* renew their strength *and* power; they shall lift their wings *and* mount up [close to God] as eagles [mount up to the sun]; they shall run and not be weary, they shall walk and not faint *or* become tired.

> Colossians 1:27 - To whom God was pleased to make known how great for the Gentiles are the riches of the glory of this mystery, which is Christ within and among you, the Hope of [realizing the] glory.

22

JESUS IN THE SURRENDER

Today, I was forced to relinquish my plans to partake in activities I love. I simply do not have the strength to push past this wretched tiredness. I know it is wise that I rest, but idleness does not agree with me. I would like to maintain my regular schedule.

You know my heart and what I need, Lord. I **Invite You In** so I can trust You have my best interests at heart. I discern the difference when I resign to something and when I surrender to it. To surrender to Your Way and Your Will is to relinquish my stiff-necked methods to your Loving Sovereignty. Resigning dictates that I trust in *myself* with all *my* heart and lean on *my* own understanding –in all *my* ways, acknowledge *myself* and make *my* paths straight. My, my, my! This emphasis on MY will is the total opposite of YOUR will for me. In fact, resignation to my will in my circumstances makes me feel alone, uncared for and angry. Therefore, I must insert Your name into this verse of Truth and not my own.

As I **Invite You In**, I lean on Your Truth, receive Your strength and place my trust in You.

Proverbs 3:5-6 - Trust in the LORD with all your heart and do not lean on your own understanding. In all your ways acknowledge Him, and He will make your paths straight.

23

JESUS IN THE DISAPPOINTMENT

Seemingly, I am imprisoned in a sea of fear. I give that to You, Jesus, and ask You to give me what You want me to have in exchange for it because You took care of my fear at the cross when you took my old man and exchanged it for your glorious LIFE. I **Invite You In**

> ...to be my God (Who) will liberally supply (fill to the full) my every need according to His riches in glory in Christ Jesus (Philippians 4:19)

As I **Invite You In**, You remind me of what You are designing in and through me.

> Romans 5:3-5 - ...but we also exult in our tribulations...tribulation brings about perseverance; perseverance, proven character; proven character, hope; and hope does not disappoint, because the love of God has been poured out within our hearts through the Holy Spirit... (NASB)

24

JESUS IN THE DOUBTS

Lord, I know I concern myself with so much that You have already taken care of. I am experiencing and now believing that You know my heart's desires and one of them is to keep my focus on You instead of my circumstances. I guess I forget that I have the heart and mind of Christ. Your desires are mine. I **Invite You In** to bring Truth to any lie or doubt that would keep me from believing Your Word. I'm so glad You're holding onto me. I do have strength to believe, and that is all You ask of me. Thank You!

As I **Invite You In**, I see fruit produced in believing.

> Isaiah 26:3 - You will guard him and keep him in perfect and constant peace whose mind [both its inclination and its character] is stayed on You, because he commits himself to You, leans on You, and hopes confidently in You.

> Psalms 138:8 - The Lord will perfect that which concerns me; Your mercy and loving-kindness, O Lord, endure forever—forsake not the works of Your own hands.

> 1 Corinthians 2:16b - ...But we have the mind of Christ. (NASB)

25

JESUS IN THE WEAKNESS

I grew up believing strength was my strongest virtue. It didn't compute that I was operating in my own strength. I hope that I never succumb to that again. I have no resources within myself to be strong, better, more accomplished, etc. I understand that my weakness is attractive to You, Jesus, because You can work with all my antics out of the way. It is not that You were unable to accomplish this previously, but I finally understand that I am now poised to cooperate! I fully grasp that Your strength is made perfect in my weakness. I **Invite You In** as I yield to You and realize that You do not want my strength, You want to be my Strength. I am so thankful!

As I **Invite You In**, I find You are all the Superman I need.

> Isaiah 30:15 - For thus said the Lord God, the Holy One of Israel: In returning [to Me] and resting [in Me] you shall be saved; in quietness and in [trusting] confidence shall be your strength...

> Philippians 4:13 - I have strength for all things in Christ Who empowers me [I am ready for anything and equal to anything through Him Who infuses inner strength into me; I am self-sufficient in Christ's sufficiency].

26

JESUS IN THE DOUBTS

I am reflecting on what could be. I know that You, Jesus, are my Eternal Life and personally that means my past, present and future are in You. My finite mind cannot wrap around the totality of this Truth. I must believe without understanding. This means that I trust You for the past, the present and the future. My hope is for You to take care of me in this long illness. Please use it for my good because I cannot imagine how You do that! I do not need understanding, I just need You, Jesus. I **Invite You** In to my doubts, fears and decisions. I relinquish to You the hearts of my loved ones standing with me and the myriad of people praying for me that I do not even know. What a humbling thought.

As I **Invite You In**, I find Your assurance.

> I John 5:20 - And we know that the Son of God has come, and he has given us understanding so that we can know the true God. And now we live in fellowship with the true God because we live in fellowship with his Son, Jesus Christ. He is the only true God, and he is eternal life. (NLT)

> Romans 8:28 - We are assured and know that [God being a partner in their labor] all things work together and are [fitting into a plan] for good to and for those who love God and are called according to [His] design and purpose.

27

JESUS IN THE PLAN

In past crises in my life, I have come to You believing that nothing can thwart Your plan, God. I have trusted Your Word. I know that I am experiencing the Truth of that once more. Cancer. It is difficult to believe that such a devastating disease could be part of Your plan, Lord. However, to get through this part of the journey, I can do all things through Christ who strengthens me. Furthermore, You reveal to me it is YOU Who can do all things. It is difficult to push these crazy feelings out of the way. I **Invite You In** today to all the confusion, unhappiness, fear and dread of this disease, this deep grief. I believe You want my honesty and You want me in Your lap telling You just how I feel. Is that intimacy? I sure hope so, because here I come. I want All that You are today and none of these feelings. Please exchange them afresh and anew because I have Your Life living in me! I have nowhere else to go with this. I will be ecstatic when I only desire Your Presence!

As I **Invite You In**, You reveal that the exchange is in Christ alone and You are willing to come to me with mercy that is new every morning. This reminds me of what You want me to have instead of settling for emotions that suffocate me.

Isaiah 61:3
Job 42:2

28

JESUS IN THE TURMOIL

I am witnessing a pattern to my emotional roller coaster ride, Jesus. On days when I feel strong, I plug right into Hebrews 13:20-21,

> Now the God of peace, who brought up from the dead the great Shepherd of the sheep through the blood of the eternal covenant, even Jesus our Lord, equip you in every good thing to do His will, working in us that which is pleasing in His sight, through Jesus Christ, to whom be the glory forever and ever. Amen.

Please God, do not let my feelings determine how positive my day will be. I'm asking because I do not even have the energy to choose what I want. I want You and the Truth of this verse every moment of every day. I **Invite You In**. Take me off the roller coaster! I feel like the Psalmist today as I **Invite You In** to minister to my heart.

As I **Invite You In**, I am called to trust and experience every benefit of Psalm 13 and Psalm 23.

> Psalms 23:2-3 - You have bedded me down in lush meadows, you find me quiet pools to drink from. True to your word, you let me catch my breath and send me in the right direction. (MSG)

29

JESUS IN THE TURMOIL

My physical ups and downs leave me so frustrated. On one end of the spectrum, I have health to seemingly cruise ninety miles an hour; on the other end, I sit in this chair day after day feeling totally useless. How much worth am I earning from doing? This "queen of do" certainly can't "do" anything now.

I know my worth is in You, Jesus, ministering or sitting. It is not about what I can do or have done. It is all about what You have accomplished for me. All the necessary work to make us worthy is finished in Your economy because of the cross. I **Invite You In** to this pain of feeling useless. I know this is a lie. It just feels so real.

As I **Invite You In**, I seek your face. I know if I seek You, You will be found.

> Psalms 27:7-8 - Hear, O Lord, when I cry aloud; have mercy and be gracious to me and answer me! You have said, Seek My face (inquire for and require My presence as your vital need). My heart says to You, Your face (Your Presence), Lord, will I seek, inquire for, and require (of necessity and on the authority of Your Word.

> Jeremiah 29:13 - You will seek Me and find Me when you search for Me with all your heart. (NASB)

30

Jesus in the Discontentment

I settle into quiet days of inactivity. I need Your direction, Lord, to do what it is You want: to follow Your lead, to stay on track mentally and emotionally, not falling prey to self-pity, depression, circumstances and loneliness. Here it is, my opportunity to learn contentment. I **Invite You In**. I do not know how to be content amidst all of this. You will have to take the lead. No, You must accomplish this for me. Please bring me to a place of rest and contentment. I certainly cannot attain this on my own.

As I **Invite You In,** I ask You to bring to fruition Your perfect purpose.

> Philippians 4:11 - Not that I am implying that I was in any personal want, for I have learned how to be content (satisfied to the point where I am not disturbed or disquieted) in whatever state I am.

> Isaiah 30:15 - For thus said the Lord God, the Holy One of Israel: In returning [to Me] and resting [in Me] you shall be saved; in quietness and in [trusting] confidence shall be your strength...

> Psalms 25:5 - Guide me in Your truth and faithfulness and teach me, for You are the God of my salvation; for You [You only and altogether] do I wait [expectantly] all the day long.

31

JESUS IN THE DISCOURAGEMENT

My appetite or lack of is still a struggle, Jesus. Yes, food is needed for my physical body, but never have I needed You more as my Bread of Life and my Living Water as I do now. I know I need to eat to keep up my strength, but I need You to minister to my soul—my mind, will and emotions. The Truth will continue to set me free from these overwhelming feelings. It is very difficult to fight when my body is one massive ache. Today, I **Invite You In** to "...perfect that which concerns me!" This is another glorious promise You have made me. Keep that promise today, as only You can, please, Jesus!

As I **Invite You In,** You encourage me as my Living Water and Bread of Life—Eternal Food!

> John 7:38 - He who believes in Me [who cleaves to and trusts in and relies on Me] as the Scripture has said, From his innermost being shall flow [continuously] springs and rivers of living water.

> Psalms 36:9 - For with You is the fountain of life; In Your light we see light.

> John 6:35 - I am the Bread of Life. He who comes to Me will never be hungry, and he who believes in and cleaves to and trusts in and relies on Me will never thirst any more (at any time).

32

JESUS IN THE DISCONTENTMENT

Jesus, I am struggling with this idea of learning to be content. Is contentment really a possibility? Paul did it with the skin beaten off his back, singing praise songs at that! He is my example as he wrote the Epistles, primarily from prison. I imagine this bloody figure, a dungeon, rats and spoiled food. From this image I can learn it is not necessarily the outward that brings contentment. It is, most assuredly, what the mind is set on that allows feelings and actions to follow. Paul, indeed, focused with his mind of Christ.

I feel imprisoned in this house, this body, this treatment. It seems cancer, sickness, grief is winning! Is it cancer in my body or my soul—mind, will and emotions—that I should be concerned about, Jesus? I **Invite You In** to be all that I need in this turmoil of the body and soul. Remind me I have the mind of Christ.

As I **Invite You In,** I hear You whisper…

> John 14:27 - Peace I give to you. Not as the world gives, give I unto You. Let not your hearts be troubled, neither let them be afraid. (Stop allowing yourselves to be agitated and disturbed; and do not permit yourselves to be fearful and intimidated and cowardly and unsettled.)

33

JESUS IN THE DISAPPOINTMENT

Today has been a difficult day. I know in You "we (I) live and move and have our (my) being." (Parentheses mine) Yes, me, one with You, Jesus. As I exist in this cancerous, sick body of nausea, weakness and pain, I need the reality of that verse. I **Invite You In** to take me far beyond the natural to protect me from feeling as if I am unloved, uncared for and vulnerable to the lies that You are not there for me. I know that You know just how much I am struggling today. If I focus on You, I know that I will not be as likely to fall into disappointment and self-pity. I **Invite You In** to take my eyes and turn them on You and not this struggle.

As I **Invite You In**, You are there to bring me back to the Truth, because today I feel like forlorn Job.

> Job 7:3 - So am I allotted months of futile [suffering], and [long] nights of misery are appointed to me.

> Psalms 40:1-3 - I waited patiently for the LORD; And He inclined to me and heard my cry. He brought me up out of the pit of destruction, out of the miry clay, And He set my feet upon a rock making my footsteps firm. He put a new song in my mouth, a song of praise to our God; Many will see and fear And will trust in the LORD. (NASB)

34

JESUS IN THE BATTLE

Does anyone fully grasp Your magnitude and might, Jesus? I want to receive the Truth of that amidst the vortex that is sucking the life out of me. I open my heart to all of You! I want, no, I need, no, I must know You in all places: mentally, emotionally, physically, and spiritually. You are LIFE! How do I experience that in what feels like death to all I have known as life? I **Invite You In** to all that is fighting against me in what I know of Truth. Come, Lord Jesus.

As I **Invite You In**, You speak to me about what True Life is. It is found only in resting and abiding in You!

> John 6:63 - It is the Spirit Who gives life [He is the Life-giver]; the flesh conveys no benefit whatever [there is no profit in it]. The words (truths) that I have been speaking to you are spirit and life.

> 1 John 2:16 - For all that is in the world, the lust of the flesh and the lust of the eyes and the boastful pride of life, is not from the Father, but is from the world.

> Isaiah 30:15 - For thus said the Lord God, the Holy One of Israel: In returning [to Me] and resting [in Me] you shall be saved; in quietness and in [trusting] confidence shall be your strength...

35

JESUS IN THE QUANDARY

What is a good day? Is it accomplishing much as opposed to paralysis of mind and soul? Today, I have energy to go about my business while enjoying free and easy breathing; there is no pain. I think I may have the strength to entertain and enjoy a friend. All the while I ask myself, what is Life? I **Invite You In**, Lord, to this "good" day. I know that being able to breathe well, having a little extra strength and energy, is not True Life. I do not want to settle for that. You are my Life. Minister to this place in my heart. I desire to experience Your Presence amidst all this cancer of the body and soul.

As I **Invite You In**, You impart True Life to me; and I know True Life is in the Spirit and we are in union. You desire to bear that Fruit through me, even amidst the sickness.

> Ephesians 5:9 - For the fruit (the effect, the product) of the Light or the Spirit [consists] in every form of kindly goodness, uprightness of heart, and trueness of life.

> Philippians 1:11 - May you abound in and be filled with the fruits of righteousness (of right standing with God and right doing) which come through Jesus Christ (the Anointed One), to the honor and praise of God [that His glory may be both manifested and recognized].

36

JESUS IN THE IDOLS

Every day I know that I bow to something. I realize amidst this illness that my idol can quickly become my comfort. You tell me in Your Living Word You are my Comfort, Jesus. It is not just something that You are going to give me. My Comfort is You! I must choose to totally depend on You today, every day. I long for the everlasting Comfort You offer. I do not want to settle for just a comfortable, better than what I've had lately day. I want to know the Trueness of all that You have for me. I **Invite You In** so that Comfort has a new definition for me—You!

As I **Invite You In,** You begin to turn my eyes from my idols back to You.

> Jonah 2:8 - Those who pay regard to false, useless, and worthless idols forsake their own [Source of] mercy and loving-kindness.

> 1 John 5:21 - Little children, keep yourselves from idols (false gods)--[from anything and everything that would occupy the place in your heart due to God, from any sort of substitute

> 1 Thessalonians 1:9 - For they themselves volunteer testimony concerning us, telling what an entrance we had among you, and how you turned to God from [your] idols to serve a God Who is alive and true and genuine,

37

JESUS IN THE PLAN

One day I am going to thank the author, Ann Voskamp, for enlightening me in so many areas of my faith walk. I am seeking fullness of life in my present state of cancer (of body and soul) and she states that the fullness of life is gratitude for everything, because even the "ugly beautiful"[1], as she calls it, leads to grace and joy. This encourages me to framework this difficult time in Your love, Jesus—not to understand this horror, but to accept it. I remember being taught that I do not need to understand anything to accept it as part of Your plan for my life. However, I do have to understand that what I am accepting is not just Your plan for me, but Your unfathomable love for me. I acknowledge that union with You enables me to think eternally, supernaturally, all past what I can see. I need You today to do that! I **Invite You In** because I desire to see through your eternal eyes.

As I **Invite You In**, I ask You to open my spirit eye to what You see.

> Deuteronomy 29:29 - The secret things belong unto the Lord our God, but the things which are revealed belong to us and to our children forever...

> Ephesians 5:20 - At all times and for everything giving thanks in the name of our Lord Jesus Christ to God the Father.

38

JESUS IN THE UNBELIEF

The verses in John 6:28-29 profoundly speak to me lately? I live by their Truth encapsulated in this one word—believe! Did chemo and pain killing drugs destroy the part of my brain that believes You, Jesus? I am certain that belief is that address in our being where God's unconditional Love, Joy, Peace, Comfort, Healing, etc. is made real. I remember that much today! All of You, Christ, and Your union with me zoom into reality when I believe You are Who You say You are and I am who You say I am. This does not seem to be dependent on anything except You alone. I believe. Help me in my unbelief today. I **Invite You In.**

As I **Invite You In** to enter this terrible brain fog, You delight in ministering to me, Spirit to spirit.

> John 6:28-29 - They then said, What are we to do, that we may [habitually] be working the works of God? [What are we to do to carry out what God requires?] Jesus replied, This is the work (service) that God asks of you: that you believe in the One Whom He has sent [that you cleave to, trust, rely on, and have faith in His Messenger].

39

JESUS IN THE TURMOIL

No truer words were ever spoken than these: "Trauma's storm can mask the Christ and feelings can lie."[1] as penned by Ann Voskamp. I cannot believe how quickly I succumb to lies and feelings. I know that part of my journey and quest is to know Jesus as my Enough. My emotions are desperately attempting to steal His Joy and beauty from me. My cup runneth over with blessings: love and prayers of friends, breathing without a struggle, love of family, provision, revelation of His eternal vision by His Spirit, a desire to come to Him; pure Grace and Mercy every day.

These blessings come from Your two promises to me, Lord: "Grace and peace be multiplied to you in the knowledge of God and of Jesus our Lord; seeing that His divine power has granted to us everything pertaining to life and godliness, through the true knowledge of Him who called us by His own glory and excellence (2 Peter 1:2-3); He who did not withhold or spare even His own son but gave Him up for us all, will He not also with Him freely and graciously give us all [other] things?" (Romans 8:32)

I **invite You In,** simply, **Invite You In**, Jesus. I have nothing to give. I am ready to receive.

(To the reader: Here is another invitation for a most personal time with Jesus to minister to you, right where you are. I know from experience on days like this, that is exactly what He wants to do. Let Him! **Invite Him In!**)

40

JESUS IN THE DARKNESS

Once again, Ann Voskamp saves the day. Thank you, Lord, for revealing to her the Truth of Moses being tucked into the cleft of the rock. She shared, "When it's dark, it's only because God has tucked me in the cleft of a rock and covered me, protected, with His hand...Dark is the holiest ground, the glory passing by. In the blackest, God is closest, at work, forging His perfect and right will. Though it is black and we can't see and our world seems to be free-falling and we feel utterly alone, Christ is most present to us... ."[1] Is that true, Lord? If I can stop focusing on my circumstances long enough to look by faith and believe, I know it is. I need You, Jesus! I **Invite You In** to bring revelation and light to this darkness.

As I **Invite You In**, I choose to experience You as my Light in this season of darkness.

> Exodus 33:22 - And while My glory passes by, I will put you in a cleft of the rock and cover you with My hand until I have passed by.

> 2 Corinthians 4:6 - For God, who said, "Light shall shine out of darkness," is the One who has shone in our hearts to give the Light of the knowledge of the glory of God in the face of Christ. (NASB)

41

JESUS IN THE BATTLE

I realize in looking at the bleakness of the present moment I can keep my eyes glued to the movie screen of my own life or I can choose to rest in You, Lord and the healing Word You have spoken through Psalm 41. Whether my healing is for now or heaven, it really does not matter. My battle, the war waged between feelings verses Truth, is real in this present, vivid moment. You want me, all of me, to rest in You, not in how or what You are going to do, but simply You. I do not want to refuse any part of the gift of healing in my body or soul. Today feels like a soul-healing day, where my mind, will and emotions are being brought to Truth—FREEDOM!

Jesus, I **Invite You In** to carry me through.

As I **Invite You In**, thank You for reminding me of Your eternal view. I know that as You spoke to David, You also speak to me.

> Psalms 125:1 – Those who trust in, lean on, and confidently hope in the Lord are like Mount Zion, which cannot be moved but abides and stands fast forever.

> 1 Peter 1:21 - Through Him you believe in (adhere to, rely on) God, Who raised Him up from the dead and gave Him honor and glory, so that your faith and hope are [centered and rest] in God.

42

JESUS IN THE QUANDARY

I am surrounded by people who are succumbing to the flu. I even tested positive for it and am taking my homeopathic remedy to protect me. This is not my idea of abundant living. A rich overflowing existence is simply Christ living His Life through me. Therefore, all difficulties and joys are the basic elements of abundant life. Where does the flu fit in then? I can claim this adversity as a simple avenue by which the Father can bring me to total dependence on Him.

Standing firm in this Truth requires me to take my eyes off my circumstances and believe that You, Jesus, have given me everything for Life and Godliness—Your eternal perspective. I need You to carry me beyond this! Through the flu, or cancer or any unnerving trauma that comes my way, I **Invite You In** to change my earthly perspective!

As I **Invite You In,** no matter what comes my way, I need You to reveal that You are Abundant Life.

> 2 Peter 1:3 - For His divine power has bestowed upon us all things that [are requisite and suited] to life and godliness, through the [full, personal] knowledge of Him Who called us by and to His own glory and excellence (virtue).

> John 10:10 - "The thief comes only to steal and kill and destroy; I came that they may have life, and have it abundantly."

43

JESUS IN THE STRUGGLE

I saw one of my chemo buddies almost crash today when she was switched to a new protocol...too much for her heart. I believe this entire process is about to crash my heart as well, not to make light of anything that happened today.

With everything I have and am holding onto, which is You, Lord, I acknowledge that joy is not some feel good something. The fruit of the Spirit is Joy. That is not just something You are going to give me—it is You in me! This makes me a joyful person no matter the circumstance. I **Invite You In** so that I can experience this Joy in the midst of what feels like a joyless time. I choose JOY! I choose YOU!

As I **Invite You In**, I am reminded of Truth, the Joy-giving Truth!

> Luke 6:21 - Blessed (happy— with life-joy and satisfaction in God's favor and salvation, apart from your outward condition—and to be envied) are you who hunger and seek with eager desire now, for you shall be filled and completely satisfied! Blessed (happy— with life-joy and satisfaction in God's favor and salvation, apart from your outward condition—and to be envied) are you who weep and sob now, for you shall laugh!

44

JESUS IN THE TURMOIL

Am I living life to the fullest right here where I am? My schedule is mundane but must my relationship with You be so, Jesus? Although deeply concerned, I am grateful that, for today, I am not in much pain; I can breathe with relative ease. This is a quiet time for sure. Show me how You want to minister to my heart, right here where You have me. What more can I ask for but a more intimate relationship where You reveal Your love to me? Psalm 41:10, "...be gracious to me and raise me up and then I will know." I **Invite You In** to this turmoil in my thinking.

As I **Invite You In**, You whisper, "Receive my Love." This is an invitation to know You in the depths of my being because You are Love. You are Truth.

> John 8:32 - And you will know the Truth, and the Truth will set you free.
>
> Philippians 1:9 - And this I pray: that your love may abound yet more and more and extend to its fullest development in knowledge and all keen insight [that your love may display itself in greater depth of acquaintance and more comprehensive discernment]...

45

JESUS IN THE PLAN

I want to know Your fiery, passionate love, Jesus. I want this to be the sweetest time ever. Come to me, Lover of my soul, Jesus. Come to dispel the feelings of loneliness, abandonment, vulnerability, unimportance, and ostracization. I **Invite You In** to minister to my heart. The Truth is: You are with me; I am never alone; I am so important that You died because You did not want to live without me; I was included in Your incredible plan. I need to focus on You, not the disappointments because of the expectations I have placed on the way I want my healing. Your Way versus mine.

As I **Invite You In**, You remind me to focus on the Truth that You are The Way and the Lover of my soul.

> Psalms 45:10-15 - Listen to me, O royal daughter; take to heart what I say. Forget your people and your homeland far away. For your royal husband delights in your beauty; honor him, for he is your lord. The princess of Tyre will shower you with gifts. The wealthy will beg your favor. The bride, a princess, waits within her chamber, dressed in a gown woven with gold. In her beautiful robes, she is led to the king, accompanied by her bridesmaids. What a joyful, enthusiastic procession as they enter the king's palace! (NLT)

46

JESUS IN THE DISAPPOINTMENT

I want Author Ann Voskamp's mindset of thankfulness when I don't know what to think. I desire to give thanks for feeling better, but that is not the case at this moment. This is post-chemo week which historically leaves me reeling in oppressive nausea and general malaise. My hope is to experience the revelation knowledge of Jesus growing and growing in me. I can be thankful for that. Hurt, disappointment and discouragement seem to be the walls that constantly stand in the way of my experiencing LIFE in Him. I do not want to live in that mire, dependent on feelings that are so deceptive. I know I have always waited on circumstances to deliver me, but the feelings attached to them cause my footing to be so unsure. This cancer battle does not change.

From day to day, I see my body losing ground, but this particular battle appears to be cancer of the soul (mind, will and emotions), which can only manifest in unbelief. Jesus, I **Invite You In** to cure this. As **I Invite You In,** I choose to believe Your unchangeable nature, attributes and character are mine to experience because I am one with You. I know focusing on You will bring clarity to my soul revealing not only Your depth but what You want me to experience each moment. A portion of this intimacy is pouring out how I feel while enjoying a loving relationship with You. I thank You for Life and Godliness in abundance, Your promises to me.

Intimacy - *in to me see*, my Lord. My circumstance may not change, but I yield to focus on You.

2 Corinthians 9:15 - Now thanks be to God for His Gift, [precious] beyond telling [His indescribable, inexpressible, free Gift]! (Jesus Christ!)

Ephesians 5:20 - At all times and for everything giving thanks in the name of our Lord Jesus Christ to God the Father.

1 Corinthians 15:22 - For just as [because of their union of nature] in Adam all people die, so also [by virtue of their union of nature] shall all in Christ be made alive.

Ephesians 2:5 - Even when we were dead (slain) by [our own] shortcomings and trespasses, He made us alive together in fellowship and in union with Christ; [He gave us the very life of Christ Himself, the same new life with which He quickened Him, for] it is by grace (His favor and mercy which you did not deserve) that you are saved (delivered from judgment and made partakers of Christ's salvation).

Colossians 3:15 - And let the peace (soul harmony which comes) from Christ rule (act as umpire continually) in your hearts [deciding and settling with finality all questions that arise in your minds, in that peaceful state] to which as [members of Christ's] one body you were also called [to live]. And be thankful (appreciative), [giving praise to God always].

47

JESUS IN THE DECEPTION

I confess that You are My Enough today, Jesus, no matter what feelings slam up against me accusingly spewing untruths. Manifest the purity of my heart in me to focus on You. Please remove all the blocks, all the lies about You that keep me from crawling into Your lap. When feelings wash over me like some torrent let loose, I know that to believe Who You say You are and who You say I am will minister to my heart. I **Invite You In.** I choose to believe.

As I **Invite You In,** I find Your faithfulness ministers to my soul.

> Habakkuk 3: 17-19 - Though the fig tree does not blossom and there is no fruit on the vines, [though] the product of the olive fails and the fields yield no food, though the flock is cut off from the fold and there are no cattle in the stalls, Yet I will rejoice in the Lord; I will exult in the [victorious] God of my salvation! The Lord God is my Strength, my personal bravery, *and* my invincible army; He makes my feet like hinds' feet and will make me to walk [not to stand still in terror, but to walk] *and* make [spiritual] progress upon my high places [of trouble, suffering, or responsibility]!
>
> Lamentations 3:23b - …great and abundant is Your stability and faithfulness.

48

JESUS IN THE DISCOURAGEMENT

I feel blue today and as I take a good look at "blue", I find that it is hidden in the uncertainty of what is going to happen. All I visualize is illness, weight loss, lack of appetite and worried faces from family and friends. I begin to wonder, is it Your job, Jesus, to fill my heart with thanksgiving? Or is thanksgiving a gift You have already bestowed upon me? I cannot see what You see. I cannot know what You know. What do I do with those soul penetrating questions? I **Invite You In** to answer them. They seem to present themselves daily!

As I **Invite You In,** I receive the Truth of Romans 15:13. HOPE is not in my healing, not in my feeling better, a good appetite, making my family and friends feel better, but in You: all that You say that You are, my Security, my Hope, My Joy, My Power and My Peace.

> Psalms 27:14 - Wait and hope for and expect the Lord; be brave and of good courage and let your heart be stout and enduring. Yes, wait for and hope for and expect the Lord.

> Psalms 33:22 - Let Your mercy and loving-kindness, O Lord, be upon us, in proportion to our waiting and hoping for You.

> Psalms 38:15 - For in You, O Lord, do I hope; You will answer, O Lord my God.

49

JESUS IN THE MUNDANE

Having family and friends nearby certainly brings variety to mundane days - a most welcome diversion. I look and I wait for change in my circumstances. I know the Truth of the New Covenant is that I am already transformed because of the finished work of the cross. As I read in Psalm 41:3, that You would turn, change and transform my bed of illness, Lord, I cling to Your words to me. All I can do is hope in You—all of Who You are and Your promises.

I **Invite You In** so I might experience all that You have for me in healing and transforming me, "…to heal my inner self, for I have sinned against You." My sin is unbelief and I know it. I turn as You turn and transform me.

As I **Invite You In,** the power of Romans 12:2 overtakes me.

> Romans 12:2 - Do not be conformed to this world (this age), [fashioned after and adapted to its external, superficial customs], but be transformed (changed) by the [entire] renewal of your mind [by its new ideals and its new attitude], so that you may prove [for yourselves] what is the good and acceptable and perfect will of God, even the thing which is good and acceptable and perfect [in His sight for you].

50

JESUS IN THE DARKNESS

On certain days, I succumb to suffering: the darkness of debilitating illness, witnessing the deterioration of my body, having no ability to maintain my household, the everyday tasks I did not even give a second thought to; each attack painfully daunting. I know that having a thankful heart takes the sting out of all the adversity. I want to see light. Light!

I **Invite You In** to manifest Yourself, Jesus, as my Light.

As I **Invite You In,** You whisper to me that Your never failing Presence lives within me to bring True Light. You are willing to open my eyes to see You. Thank You that You are, indeed, my Light of the world.

> John 8:12 - Once more Jesus addressed the crowd. He said, I am the Light of the world. He who follows Me will not be walking in the dark, but will have the Light which is Life.

> Psalms 89:15 - How blessed are the people who know the joyful sound! O LORD, they walk in the light of Your countenance.

> Ephesians 5:20 - At all times and for everything giving thanks in the name of our Lord Jesus Christ to God the Father.

51

Jesus in the Grief

It seems that I have hopped on an emotional roller coaster again. How can that happen so quickly? A good day, a bad day, back to a good day. My feelings are controlled by how well I feel and bam, that becomes my truth for the day! I guess for today I just do not get it. I am so hurt, disappointed and discouraged and it seems to be a reality I cannot escape.

Jesus, I want to experience Your Life in this place, but today, I cannot break through. Come get me Lord! I **Invite You In** because You are all that I need today. I know You are Enough. Would You nurture my heart?

As I **Invite You In**, I acknowledge Your Presence, whether I feel it or not. I can open my Bible and read and that might bring me comfort. I just do not want it to be knowledge without relationship and intimacy. Right now I need You! I have witnessed the manifestation of Your Word through other people, a praise song, the wind rustling, and a thunderstorm. How will You show Yourself to me today? Open my Spirit eyes that are so tightly bound in my feelings today. I cry out to You to break through my emotions so I can see and experience the work You have done in me.

Reader: I encourage you to go to the Lord today with your struggle and receive what His Living Word says. Listen to see what His still small voice whispers to your heart. Lies that we are tempted to believe and the feelings that accompany them need a personal exchange today. Give to Him what you are carrying and see what He wants you to have in exchange. **Invite Him In!**

2 Samuel 5:20 - And David came to Baal-perazim, and he smote them there, and said, The Lord has broken through my enemies before me, like the bursting out of great waters. So he called the name of that place Baal-perazim [Lord of breaking through].

1 Chronicles 14:11 - So [Israel] came up to Baal-perazim, and David smote [the Philistines] there. Then David said, God has broken my enemies by my hand, like the bursting forth of waters. Therefore they called the name of that place Baal-perazim [Lord of breaking through].

1 Thessalonians 5:16-18 - Be happy [in your faith] and rejoice and be glad-hearted continually (always); be unceasing in prayer [praying perseveringly]; Thank [God] in everything [no matter what the circumstances may be, be thankful and give thanks], for this is the will of God for you [who are] in Christ Jesus [the Revealer and Mediator of that will].

Isaiah 61:3 - To grant [consolation and joy] to those who mourn in Zion--to give them an ornament (a garland or diadem) of beauty instead of ashes, the oil of joy instead of mourning, the garment [expressive] of praise instead of a heavy, burdened, and failing spirit--that they may be called oaks of righteousness [lofty, strong, and magnificent, distinguished for uprightness, justice, and right standing with God], the planting of the Lord, that He may be glorified.

52

JESUS IN THE DISAPPOINTMENT

Since I am indulging in a pity party, here are my honest questions for the day, Lord. Do you hear me? Am I asking for the wrong things? Have I always? How did I end up here? I was not careless with my health or eating. I exercised so that I could be strong and healthy for whatever it was You would call me to. Even spiritually, I was sold out and surrendered to You, to go, to be, to say whatever it was You wanted. Please take the hurt and disappointment, the discouragement and this disease—all that is constantly knocking at the door of my mind. I sound like Job!!! I **Invite You In** because the self-righteousness of what I have done to prevent all this has filled my mind. I do not want to lose sight of what You have done. Come, Lord Jesus!

As I **Invite You In**, I find you whispering that You are my HOPE! My hope and focus cannot be on my circumstances—pain, weakness, or any part of this situation. It must simply be to hope in You and all that You offer me in the moment. I yield to that which takes me to Your eternal way of thinking. Keep my eyes on You amidst the hurt, fear, discouragement and disease. You are my HOPE! That means I can experience Your Life and all that it offers me this very moment: Love, Joy, Peace, Patience, Goodness, Kindness, Faithfulness, Humility and Self-control. I know that as I abide in You, the fruit of the Spirit is mine because I am in union with You. I already possess those because I have You! Unbelief is the only blockade to keep me from experiencing all You have for me. Therefore, Lord, I believe no matter what my feelings try to dictate. You are my HOPE, indeed!

John 6:28 - They then said, What are we to do, that we may [habitually] be working the works of God? [What are we to do to carry out what God requires?] Jesus replied, This is the work (service) that God asks of you: that you believe in the One Whom He has sent [that you cleave to, trust, rely on, and have faith in His Messenger].

Job 42:3, 5 - [You said to me] Who is this that darkens and obscures counsel [by words] without knowledge? Therefore [I now see] I have [rashly] uttered what I did not understand, things too wonderful for me, which I did not know...I had heard of You [only] by the hearing of the ear, but now my [spiritual] eye sees You.

Psalms 42:11 - Why are you cast down, O my inner self? And why should you moan over me and be disquieted within me? Hope in God and wait expectantly for Him, for I shall yet praise Him, Who is the help of my countenance, and my God.

Romans 15:13 - May the God of hope fill you with all joy and peace in believing [through the experience of your faith] that by the power of the Holy Spirit you will abound in hope and overflow with confidence in His promises.

53

JESUS IN THE BATTLE

Author Ann Voskamp firmly states, "Cancer can stalk you, but nothing can steal your joy unless you hand it over."[1] I understand how feelings continually creep in to take over and steal joy, as I succumb to them. There is a delicate balance between having the strength to fight those feelings and believing the Truth. All I know to do, at this point, is to feel those feelings and lift them up to You, Lord, in exchange for what You desire for me. I **Invite You In** to be real with You, trusting that You, Jesus, are going to hurt with me, cry with me and yet, Comfort me, Heal me with the exchanges You want me to experience today!

As I **Invite You In**, I am not disappointed with the presents You want to share with me. Today, I am led to understand that You will fight for me; You just want me to be still, stop striving, and believe. With You living Your life through me, I can do that.

> Exodus 14:14 - The Lord will fight for you; you need only to be still." (NIV)
>
> Psalms 46:10a - Let be and be still, and know (recognize and understand) that I am God.
>
> Psalms 91:11 - For He will give His angels [especial] charge over you to accompany and defend and preserve you in all your ways...

54

JESUS IN THE DEPRESSION

I do not relish the days when I am burdened and trapped by depression. It seems that life is passing me by. I once was very active, involved, the party initiator. Now I simply hear about the fun and the goings on. There is no fun, I am alone. I know I am never truly alone, but feelings are certainly deceptive.

Lord, fill the hours, the holes caused by emotions that feel so dark. I am not handing over my joy! My JOY is in You! I am simply asking You to clear my vision today to see far beyond what I feel. I **Invite You In** to do just that—me and You—a party of sorts!

As I **Invite You In**, You whisper that You are fully present with me, ALWAYS! You are, once again, asking me to believe, trust, and receive what I cannot see. Please push me way past the physical discomfort, the loneliness, the aching to get back to all I have known, the fulfillment of my life. But, wait, that looming question returns. What is real LIFE? Usher in the Truth today; make it real to my soul (mind, will and emotions) that You, You, You are real LIFE. My Joy, my Healing, my Peace, my Comfort, my day is in You, no matter what I feel. Knowing that I live in union with You, Jesus, reveals to me this is not just something You will impart in the future. I already possess it. I trust the manifestation of Your fruit in me today as I **Invite You In,** even when my feelings rebel.

2 Corinthians 5:7 - For we walk by faith [we regulate our lives and conduct ourselves by our conviction or belief respecting man's relationship to God and divine things, with trust and holy fervor; thus we walk] not by sight or appearance.

Romans 5:10 - For if while we were enemies we were reconciled to God through the death of His Son, it is much more [certain], now that we are reconciled, that we shall be saved (daily delivered from sin's dominion) through His [resurrection] life.

Psalms 51:12 - Restore to me the joy of Your salvation and sustain me with a willing spirit.

Galatians 5:22 - But the fruit of the [Holy] Spirit [the work which His presence within accomplishes] is love, joy (gladness), peace, patience (an even temper, forbearance), kindness, goodness (benevolence), faithfulness, 23 - Gentleness (meekness, humility), self-control (self-restraint, continence). Against such things there is no law [that can bring a charge].

55

JESUS IN THE STRUGGLE

My hope for today is You. You tell me that everything, everything, everything concerning me will be perfected by You. I suppose I have never thought about what that means. I know I am in a struggle for my life on earth. My list of concerns seems endless. Jesus, You came to perfect these daunting worries! What that means to me is that You already know the outcome and each step leading to that end. All I need is the next step. You are more than willing to offer that to me today. Meanwhile, You are asking me to surrender to the Truth of the promise that You provide the very best. As I agree with Your eternal purpose of my being made into the image of Christ, I see that only You, in Your economy, can bring my state to any good.

I always revert to the Truth that You protect me. Immediately, my thoughts go to Psalm 41. From the beginning, You told me that You would not give me over to the enemy. Yours is the victory, no matter what! I will never be given over to the enemy! That victory is won regardless of the outcome of my illness. I **Invite You In** to minister to any doubtful place and make it real in my experience, my *ginosko* place. I am at Your mercy!

As I **Invite You In**, Your word confirms all that I question/feel today. I am reminded that all You ever ask of me is to believe in our union - Who You say You are and who You say I am!

Psalms 41:2 - The Lord will protect him (me) and keep him (me) alive; he (I) shall be called blessed in the land; and You will not deliver him (me) to the will of his (my) enemies.

Psalms 119:105 - Your word is a lamp to my feet and a light to my path.

Psalms 138:8 - The Lord will perfect that which concerns me; Your mercy and loving-kindness, O Lord, endure forever—forsake not the works of Your own hands.

John 6:28-29 - Therefore they said to Him, "What shall we do, so that we may work the works of God?" Jesus answered and said to them, "This is the work of God, that you believe in Him (Jesus) whom He (God) has sent."

56

JESUS IN THE DARKNESS

Jesus, I acknowledge that your Power dwelling inside me is shown most effective in my weakness. The ability to dress and venture out is a milestone. I have cried a river this morning. I cannot envision myself getting any better. The absence of appetite, the weight loss and overall sickness, consumes me. I cannot do this without You. I know that I don't have to because as I **Invite You In,** I believe that You are not only my Healing but also my Healer. Break forth, Oh Beauteous, Heavenly Light! I call on You as the God of Breaking Through!

As I **Invite You In**, You break through with the Light of Your words to me!

Isaiah 58:8 - Then shall your light break forth like the morning, and your healing (your restoration and the power of a new life) shall spring forth speedily; your righteousness (your rightness, your justice, and your right relationship with God) shall go before you [conducting you to peace and prosperity], and the glory of the Lord shall be your rear guard.

Isaiah 60:1 - ARISE [from the depression and prostration in which circumstances have kept you—rise to a new life]! Shine (be radiant with the glory of the Lord), for your light has come, and the glory of the Lord has risen upon you!

57

JESUS IN THE BATTLE

I know my illness could lead to my leaving this earth. My friend did not know he would go to work, be killed in a tragic accident and never hold his beautiful wife, hang out with his two sons, or rock his grandbabies ever again. He had no way of knowing it was his final hour. He is experiencing Eternal Life.

While on this earth, am I experiencing Eternal Life today, in this moment? Eternal Life is defined as You—Your nature, attributes, thoughts and ways—a person, not a place. I **Invite You In** Eternal Life.

As I **Invite You In**, You are faithful to bring me to the reality of Your Eternal Life being lived through me—now!

> 1 John 5:20 - And we know that the Son of God has come, and he has given us understanding so that we can know the true God. And now we live in fellowship with the true God because we live in fellowship with his Son, Jesus Christ. He is the only true God, and he is eternal life.

58

JESUS IN THE QUANDARY

"Good days" and "good reports" make me so happy! However, am I really experiencing the Joy that the fruit of Your Spirit brings, because Your Spirit is one with mine? I am so thankful for those "good days." I just want to be equally thankful when life is difficult. Therefore, God, I humble myself to Your Mighty Hand so that You may exalt, heal, and lift me up in Your timing. Just a tiny question, could that be real soon?

As I **Invite You In,** I find promises to minister to me. As my friend, Gregg, says, "Lord, nurture my heart."

> Psalm 30:1-4 I will extol You, O Lord, for You have lifted me up, and have not let my enemies rejoice over me. O Lord my God, I cried to You for help, and You healed me. O Lord, You have brought up my soul from Sheol ; You have kept me alive, that I would not go down to the pit. Sing praise to the Lord, you His godly ones, And give thanks to His holy name

> Psalms 16:11 - You will make known to me the path of life; In Your presence is fullness of joy; In Your right hand there are pleasures forever. (NASB)

> 1 Peter 5:6 - Therefore humble yourselves under the mighty hand of God, that He may exalt you at the proper time...

59

JESUS IN THE BATTLE

Lord, I humble myself under your Mighty Hand. I will submit to You and Your ways in my life. This submission protects me from fighting against You. In receiving Your will, I choose to allow You to walk me through this, regardless of my feelings! Thank You! I **Invite You In**!

As I **Invite You In**, You call me to look at You, not my emotions. I consider the life of King David. He understood the fight of emotions verses Truth/trust very well!

> Psalm 13:1-6 To the Chief Musician. A Psalm of David. HOW LONG will You forget me, O Lord? Forever? How long will You hide Your face from me? How long must I lay up cares within me and have sorrow in my heart day after day? How long shall my enemy exalt himself over me? Consider and answer me, O Lord my God; lighten the eyes [of my faith to behold Your face in the pitch like darkness], lest I sleep the sleep of death, Lest my enemy say, I have prevailed over him, *and* those that trouble me rejoice when I am shaken. **But I have trusted**, leaned on, *and* been confident in Your mercy *and* loving-kindness; my heart shall rejoice *and* be in high spirits in Your salvation. I will sing to the Lord, because He has dealt bountifully with me.

60

Jesus in the Weakness

One thing is for certain, I cannot count on the stability of well-being. I surrender the right to even hold onto good health. The weakness and horrible malaise some days feel like waves crashing over me. Here I am, washed up on the shore with this life-stealing disease. I do not want the physical malady to win a victory over my soul (mind, will and emotions).

Lord Jesus, I know You are fighting the battle for me. I am really trying to focus on Your gifts and be thankful for them. Gifts such as two to four hours of sleep and the ability to breathe and eat a morsel of food are priceless. This seems like such a meager list compared to my usual "wants". For now, I better receive this as my new usual! I **Invite You In** to fight this battle for me. I am far too tired.

As I **Invite You In**, You promise me...

> Exodus 14:14 – The LORD will fight for you while you [only need to] keep silent *and* remain calm.

> Proverbs 3:5-6 - Lean on, trust in, and be confident in the Lord with all your heart and mind and do not rely on your own insight or understanding. In all your ways know, recognize, and acknowledge Him, and He will direct and make straight and plain your paths.

61

Jesus in the Surrender

I surrender to pain, lethargy, an inability to stand for very long, and "I must find a chair quickly!" No, I know better than that! Jesus, You are calling me to jump off a cliff of trust into Your arms which feels like jumping into the Grand Canyon at night with no lights! Your Sovereignty is what You are calling me to believe and surrender to—Your will, Your way, Your plan. I **Invite You In** today to take the reins. What will that look like?

As I **Invite You In**, I know that I am about to discover what Your perspective of what surrender is.

> Isaiah 30:18-22 - Therefore the LORD longs to be gracious to you, And therefore He waits on high to have compassion on you…He will surely be gracious to you at the sound of your cry; when He hears it, He will answer you. Although the Lord has given you bread of privation and water of oppression, He, your Teacher will no longer hide Himself, but your eyes will behold your Teacher. Your ears will hear a word behind you, "This is the way, walk in it," whenever you turn to the right or to the left. And you will defile your graven images overlaid with silver, and your molten images plated with gold. You will scatter them as an impure thing, and say to them, "Be gone!"

62

JESUS IN THE SURRENDER

Truth. My surrender means blind faith. Lord, I surrender to Your will and way and I am not guaranteed anything that I want. You will give me what I need, a big major difference. I know You, above all, understand my mule blinders' focus. I want healing, health, my "life" back. Furthermore, Your sovereign Divine design ordains that You are Life and every day I am being saved by it. I refuse earthly joy. You are my Joy—You are my Peace—You are my All in All—You are my Enough. Ann Voskamp states, "It takes 20 minutes for the body to realize it's full of food. How long does it take the soul to realize that Your Life is full?"[1] Indeed! I **Invite You In** to this moment so that I can experience Your Life being lived through me and the fullness of it! What will I experience?

As I **Invite You In** I believe with all certainty that in this moment and the moments to come, You will show Yourself faithful. Come, Lord Jesus!

> 2 Corinthians 5:7 - It's what we trust in but don't yet see that keeps us going. (MSG)

> Romans 5:10 - For if while we were enemies we were reconciled to God through the death of His Son, it is much more [certain], now that we are reconciled, that we shall be saved (daily delivered from sin's dominion) through His [resurrection] life.

63

JESUS IN THE DARKNESS

I experienced a miracle today. As time has progressed since cancer diagnosis, I began to believe the lie that I could no longer enjoy or consume a full meal. I prepared dinner and when I served my portion, I heard a voice whisper in my head, "I can't eat that!" What? Although it sounded a lot like my voice, I recognized the voice of the enemy because of the lie attached. I renounced any spirit that tried to come against me. Guess what?! I ate every bit of my dinner. That is the miracle! I cannot believe I would listen to such deception. I am thankful!

Unfortunately, with every victory there seems to be another load to bear. I know that if I am to experience Your Joy, Jesus, then I must also experience the reality of this painful road I travel, including battles concerning the food I eat. I have cried out to You to see Your Hand. You have imparted Psalms 41, 21, 103 and now 30. Yet, I cannot see past my face! This chair, these walls, the pleasures I enjoy in this life…gone. My focus, what focus? This is even a day when I am hard pressed to focus on You. It is very difficult when feelings and reality are dim. I know! You are light! I **Invite You In** to this dark place. What do I need to see? What do I need to experience? I need to experience You. I know the only things that can cause me to stumble are my own flesh (complete with believing the lies), the world (eyes off You and onto things and circumstances that might make me feel better) and the enemy (who is a liar).

As I **Invite You In**, I begin to experience Your Light and Life when I compare the deceptions to Your Truth!

John 1:4-5 - In Him was Life, and the Life was the Light of men. And the Light shines on in the darkness, for the darkness has never overpowered it [put it out or absorbed it or appropriated it, and is unreceptive to it].

John 1:9 - There it was—the true Light [was then] coming into the world [the genuine, perfect, steadfast Light] that illumines every person.

John 10:10 - The thief comes only in order to steal and kill and destroy. I came that they may have and enjoy life, and have it in abundance (to the full, till it overflows).

1 John 2:15-17 - Do not love or cherish the world or the things that are in the world. If anyone loves the world, love for the Father is not in him. For all that is in the world--the lust of the flesh [craving for sensual gratification] and the lust of the eyes [greedy longings of the mind] and the pride of life [assurance in one's own resources or in the stability of earthly things]--these do not come from the Father but are from the world [itself]. And the world passes away and disappears, and with it the forbidden cravings (the passionate desires, the lust) of it; but he who does the will of God and carries out His purposes in his life abides (remains) forever.

64

JESUS IN THE DARKNESS

What I believe is a true turning point for me emotionally has come by way of something I have already referred to in Ann Voskamp's book, *One Thousand Gifts*. As mentioned earlier she states that when it gets dark, it is only because You tucked me in the cleft of the Rock. Glory! It really seems as if You abandoned me, but the exact opposite is at work here. Emotions verses Truth. Feels as if You have abandoned me equals You are closer than my next breath. Ann further states that, "In the blackest, You are the closest, at work forging Your perfect and right will."[1] This took my breath away because of a vision You gave me as I lay on my Doctor's table. In that vision:

> *Following the removal of the enemy's talons, I saw You coming at me with a majestic cloak. You utterly enveloped me within; You totally hid me. In that embrace, I felt so loved and cared for. Words cannot explain the depth of my healing, the extent of Your Grace. In that darkness, the ethereal light of Your Presence gave light to the darkness and I was not afraid.*

No wonder I was blind and in the dark! I was completely consumed with seeing: healing, tumors shrinking, weight loss, weight gain, good appetite. When all along, Jesus, it was Your deepest desire for me to rest and be consumed by Your Presence, contradicting that unseen, seemingly dark, devoid-of-feeling place. It is pure Love that I am to experience from You. Amazing! I'll ponder all that as I **Invite You In**.

As I **Invite You In,** I simply hear...

Exodus 33:21-22 - And the Lord said, Behold, there is a place beside Me, and you shall stand upon the rock, and while My glory passes by, I will put you in a cleft of the rock and cover you with My hand until I have passed by.

John 8:12 - Once more Jesus addressed the crowd. He said, I am the Light of the world. He who follows Me will not be walking in the dark, but will have the Light which is Life.

2 Corinthians 5:7 - for we walk by faith, not by sight— (NASB)

65

JESUS IN THE FEAR

I continue to ponder what it means to be hidden in Your Love, Jesus. I reflect on what I alluded to earlier when Ann Voskamp states, "Trauma's storm can mask the Christ and feelings can lie."[1] This statement reflects the battle which rages in my mind: feelings versus Truth. Jesus, I believe Your Word is perfect and it bears a perfect love which drives out fear. Those that are desperately ill, whether manifested by physical illness or a malady of the soul (mind, will and emotions), are full of fear. I am afraid. It is not that I do not want to wake up in Your arms, Jesus, but my proverbial bucket list is what I am hanging onto: watching grandchildren grow up, coming of age to get married, having babies of their own. I am young enough to experience all that. In fact, I already have. I believe my hesitation to let go is the cause of this fear. Am I experiencing heaven here on earth today? The answer to that question is masked which unleashes so many fearful feelings; thus, I do not feel hidden in Your Love. Pastor and Author, Dr. Andrew Farley has written a book, *Heaven Is Now*[2]. It reveals the Truth that we are in Christ and have eternal eyes, union with Christ, the Love and Life of Christ, NOW! I **Invite You In** to continue to hide me in Your perfect Love and minister to my fears.

Joseph Prince states, "I stand on no-curse ground today where disease and poverty have a claim, but I stand on the blessed ground of Jesus Who has healed me and delivered me."[3]

As I **Invite You In**, by faith I focus on Your Perfect Love and it drives out my fears and settles the dilemma of my soul.

Exodus 33:22 - And while My glory passes by, I will put you in a cleft of the rock and cover you with My hand until I have passed by.

Hebrews 13:8 - Jesus Christ is the same yesterday and today and forever. (NASB)

1 John 4:18 - There is no fear in love; but perfect love casts out fear, because fear involves punishment, and the one who fears is not perfected in love. (NASB)

Acts 7:33 - Then the Lord said to him, Remove the sandals from your feet, for the place where you are standing is holy ground and worthy of veneration.

1 John 5:20 - And we [have seen and] know [positively] that the Son of God has [actually] come to this world and has given us understanding and insight [progressively] to perceive (recognize) and come to know better and more clearly Him Who is true; and we are in Him Who is true--in His Son Jesus Christ (the Messiah). This [Man] is the true God and Life eternal.

66

JESUS IN THE SEARCH

Thank you, Lord, that all is not lost in chemo brain fog! A radical Truth recently returned to mind. This Truth dealt with the meaning of the phrase, "Seek My face" in Scripture. I was in a prayer session with a client one day when You, Holy Spirit, whispered "Psalm 27" to me. As I read and prayed, the Truth was revealed! "Seek My face" means to require You as a vital necessity in my life. Today, may I receive Your care, mercy, love, joy, peace and the other fruit of the Spirit? May I expect it? Of course, because I am one with You. Because You live in me, I receive vital, life-giving union. It covenants that You are not just going to have those Truths wash over me at random, but You live in me moment to moment. I **Invite You In.** I know it is safe to have intimate conversations with You.

As I **Invite You In,** I seek Your face.

> Psalms 27:8 - You have said, Seek My face [inquire for and require My presence as your vital need]. My heart says to You, Your face (Your presence), Lord, will I seek, inquire for, and require [of necessity and on the authority of Your Word].

> Jeremiah 29:13 - You will seek Me and find Me when you search for Me with all your heart.

67

JESUS IN THE GRIEF

During this nightmare season, I want the familiar, the recognizable, in a world where there is so much unfamiliarity. I know that my finite mind cannot comprehend all that You are, Jesus, as You live Your life through me. There still seems to be a cloud over my head. I know I am not experiencing all that I can with You, but I certainly do not know how to make living in the fullness of Christ seem real. What I do know is that processing feelings during this deep time of grief is what brings the reality of Your Love. I know I have everything in You, Christ Jesus. Please make known to me what You want to give me in exchange for all I am struggling with today. I **Invite You In.**

As I **Invite You In**, I know that You delight in exchanging this grief for Your good gifts.

> Isaiah 40:31 - But those who wait for the Lord [who expect, look for, and hope in Him] shall change and renew *(exchange)* their strength and power; they shall lift their wings and mount up [close to God] as eagles [mount up to the sun]; they shall run and not be weary, they shall walk and not faint or become tired. (Parentheses mine)

68

JESUS IN THE DISCOURAGEMENT

I am very short-sighted today. All I can see before me is preparing what I need for meals, snacks, drinks, etc. It is so difficult to remain focused, present and encouraged when I receive the chemo treatment that is so damaging to my physical body. I can only hope that it will heal me. I have spent so many years building up my body to stay well, so that in my latter years I could be physically strong enough to continue to answer Your call, Jesus. I know—wrong focus, shortsighted. I will have to cross that bridge of rebuilding my body when I get to it! Like Scarlett O'Hara laments, "I'll think about that tomorrow. Tomorrow is another day!"[1] All I have now is this moment. How shall I spend it? I **Invite You In.** I need to experience You! You are all I need in this moment.

As I **Invite You In,** it is not some glibness I want to experience. I want to *ginosko* You as the Joy of salvation that You have spoken to me about. Oh! I see the rest of that verse, **"...a willing spirit."** As I meet You in this place, You remind me I have that willing spirit because I am complete in You. You gave me that at salvation. You are Enough! I can always count on You!

Psalms 51:12 - Restore to me the joy of Your salvation and sustain me with **a willing spirit.** (NASB)

69

JESUS IN THE GRIEF

I feel numb. I am just going through the motions. In an extended illness, I must remember that there is a grief process. I wish the stages were sequential. I could just traverse through one and move on to the next, never to return to the one before. That is not reality. I have been in this numb, devoid-of-feelings place before. There does not seem to be a point behind what I am experiencing. That is my perspective, of course. Jesus, I need Your perspective. I need You to fight for me. I need You! I **Invite You In**.

As I **Invite You In,** You assure me You are fighting for me and above all, it does not have to be in my understanding. HMMM…Is my false god my focus on what I want and not the willingness to walk through what You want, Jesus?

> Psalms 24:7 - Lift up your heads, O you gates; and be lifted up, you age-abiding doors, that the King of glory may come in. Who is the King of glory? The Lord strong and mighty, the Lord mighty in battle.

> Psalms 40:4 - Blessed (happy, fortunate, to be envied) is the man who makes the Lord his refuge and trust...

70

JESUS IN THE ISOLATION

I have not felt well enough to attend church. A new flu season is upon us, which creates more of an alone, isolated time frame for me. Despite this time of seclusion, You have ushered me into the wonder of praising You, Jesus. I know You drew me into it. With all the whirling thoughts and feelings leading me to be so self-absorbed, I had forgotten just how powerful worship can be. Thank You for bringing me back to Your sanity. After all, I must remember that I have the mind of Christ! It is certainly the only escape route when I feel discouraged and abandoned and lonely. What an incredible delight it is to enter immediately into Your Presence, Lord. I must remember that the only way to really find myself is to totally focus on finding You in the moment; that will keep those nagging, fleshly, enemy thoughts quelled. I **Invite You In** to quieten my soul.

As I **Invite You In**, You reveal what builds that protective wall against the enemy!

> Hebrews 4:16 - Therefore let us draw near with confidence to the throne of grace, so that we may receive mercy and find grace to help in time of need. (NASB)

> Psalms 8:2 - Through the praise of children and infants you have established a stronghold against your enemies, to silence the foe and the avenger. (NIV)

71

JESUS IN THE TURMOIL

I am in dire need of a check point Charlie, a check-up on suffering. I want to scream about these feelings; anger always knocking at my door and the list goes on ad nauseum. I often dip into hopelessness while peering into the pit of fear and abandonment.

Each attack affects the way I envision You, Jesus. My emotions manipulate my mind constantly, tempting me to believe that I cannot trust You. I then begin to find myself straying away from You, no longer leaning on You or depending on You. I make agreements with the enemy implying, "Lord, You don't care about me or You would do something to make this better or take it from me!" There, I said it! I am not a good sufferer! However, I would far rather be in Your lap than running from and shaking an angry fist at You. I **Invite You In.** I know my healing is in You, body and soul. My spirit is already one with You, sealed and healed!

As I **Invite You In**, I find You faithful to minister to my myriad of hurts and pains. I believe that I can crawl in Your lap and be honest with my pain, as King David lamented in Psalm 13, "How long will You forget me?"

2 Corinthians 1:5 - For just as the sufferings of Christ are ours in abundance, so also our comfort is abundant through Christ. (NASB)

72

Jesus in the Battle

HOPE! This is my word for the year. Hope—not just a passing word filled with no dreams. I earnestly want to continue to live on this earth. I love my family and my ministry. I love watching my grands and great grands grow up. I desire to continue in ministry, doing what I love, teaching You, Jesus, as LIFE to those who are so hurt and broken hearted! If you ask me what my desires are, there you have it! I cannot imagine anything else right now, not even heaven. Yes, yes, yes! It is such a continual battle here. I run to You again to perfect that which concerns me. I **Invite You In** to straighten out my thoughts. Is my hope in something here or is my Hope simply You, not just **in** You, but You?

As I **Invite You In**, I ask for revelation of true hope.

> Romans 8:24-25 - For in [this] hope we were saved. But hope [the object of] which is seen is not hope. For how can one hope for what he already sees? But if we hope for what is still unseen by us, we wait for it with patience and composure.

> Romans 15:13 - May the God of your hope so fill you with all joy and peace in believing [through the experience of your faith] that by the power of the Holy Spirit you may abound and be overflowing (bubbling over) with hope.

73

JESUS IN THE FEAR

This illness invites fear and doubt. It centers my eyes on the circumstances and relationships around me. This is the wrong focus. What is produced is the appalling thought, "It's never enough!" Author Sarah Young reminds us that time trains us when we don't get an answer to our prayers. There it is, time, waiting. Am I asking You to prove Yourself, Jesus or does my believing confirm that You are Who You say You are? Either way, You are in control, Sovereign. It is clearly evident in Your Word as You relate Spirit to spirit with me. I **Invite You In** for specifics!

As I **Invite You In**, You remind me that I can rest in You and believe or else suffer in vain!

> Ephesians 3:20 - Now to Him Who, by (in consequence of) the [action of His] power that is at work within us, is able to [carry out His purpose and] do superabundantly, far over and above all that we [dare] ask or think [infinitely beyond our highest prayers, desires, thoughts, hopes, or dreams]—

> Romans 8:28 - We are assured and know that [God being a partner in their labor] all things work together and are [fitting into a plan] for good to and for those who love God and are called according to [His] design and purpose.

74

JESUS IN THE UNCERTAINTY

Scan day. This is always a day full of diverse feelings. It seems that one can rock along in treatment oblivious to what it might be doing to the body, the tumors, and the illness. But, scan day brings it all full circle. My thought process returns to the "what if's" and "if only's"—a very dangerous place. I must camp out on what I know.

God, You are the great I am and You are in the moment. No matter what that scan says, You are holding me in the palm of Your hand. You are my Security. I cannot be undone, no matter what! My focus is to be on Who You say You are, the only Truth that will call me to where I want to be, solidly wrapped in Your Peaceful (full of Peace) arms! I **Invite You In** to experience You as my All in All and my Enough as I wait, wait, wait!

Ann Voskamp wisely imparts, "What was intended to tear you apart, God intends it to set you apart. What has torn you, God makes a thin place to see glory. Whatever happens, whatever unfolds, whatever unravels, you can never be undone."[1]

As I **Invite You In**, I acknowledge that any ground but You is as shifting sand. I will fall apart, emotionally, if I live by my feelings and not the promise that You are my Rock!

Ephesians 2:20 - You are built upon the foundation of the apostles and prophets with Christ Jesus Himself the chief Cornerstone.

75

JESUS IN THE UNCERTAINTY

After a few "good" days, my body's adversary returns! Lord, You know the culprit, the enemy that does a body slam and forces out the worst of emotions. I will try to help my physical body with all that You show me, but trusting You, Jesus? That is difficult when my body is screaming! You call me to trust You: what exactly does that mean? I have all the faith I need in You alone, so, once again, You call me to believe. Trust. I pour out my feelings to You, waiting for You to whisper what You want to give me in exchange for all that I am tempted to believe and carry today. I give up my control. I recognize that You are God, not me. Having that yielded attitude is essential as I pray. You desire my focus to be on the Way You will handle all that concerns me, because You are The Way. In this I can bless You always. I **Invite You In**, because, truly, You are the only Way through this.

As I **Invite You In** and begin to pray and put my trust in You, I give You all feelings, fear and concerns. You, in Your Faithfulness, assure me that I lack no good thing.

> Psalm 34:10 - The young lions lack [food] and grow hungry, But they who seek the LORD will not lack any good thing.

> Psalm 84:11b - No good thing will He withhold from those who walk uprightly.

76

JESUS IN THE WEAKNESS

I seem to be calling out for strength these days. My physical body cannot respond to the call of fellowship, church and meeting with friends. I am unable to exercise or even prepare healthy meals.

What is necessary in this weakness? Your strength is needed, Jesus—Your strength manifested through me. Exactly how does that work? I rest in You and You manifest Your strength, (mental, emotional, and physical), to see me through each moment. I need to comprehend that throughout this journey, all I have is this moment. I **Invite You In** to be my strength, my All-in-All and my Enough today and the days ahead.

As I **Invite You In**, You remind me that You are not just going to give me strength, but You are my Strength because I am in You and You are in me! If drugs can be infused, then so can You!!! You call me to rest and trust that this moment is in Your hands. There is only one thing that would keep me from resting in You, unbelief.

> Philippians 4:13 - I have strength for all things in Christ Who empowers me [I am ready for anything and equal to anything through Him Who infuses inner strength into me; I am self-sufficient in Christ's sufficiency].

77

JESUS IN THE LAMENT

Jesus, thank you that we are one in spirit. Today, I take on Your strength and stamina. I ask for You: to stop this weight loss; for clean results from the tests and scan; for the manifestation of Psalm 41 in my life. Hope: mine is You.

Author Sarah Young motivates her readers to rejoice in the relief of being fully understood. Furthermore, author Ann Voskamp, explains during an interview that a lament is different from a complaint. Lament can express my personal feelings to You but at the same time acknowledge Your goodness, benevolence and Sovereignty, as You allow these things to conform us into the image of Christ. Nothing is lost; it is all Grace! I **Invite You In** to hear my lament.

As I **Invite You In**, I hear Your Truth through Your Word.

> Psalms 41:1-4 - How blessed is he who considers the helpless; The LORD will deliver him in a day of trouble. The LORD will protect him and keep him alive, And he shall be called blessed upon the earth; And do not give him over to the desire of his enemies. The LORD will sustain him upon his sickbed; In his illness, You restore him to health. As for me, I said, "O LORD, be gracious to me; Heal my soul, for I have sinned against You." Lord, be merciful and gracious to me; heal my inner self, for I have sinned against You.

78

JESUS IN THE PURPOSE

There do not appear to be any shortcuts while being crafted into the image of Jesus Christ. We are His handiwork, after all. Author Sarah Young relays the words of Jesus when she states, "I am leading you along the high road, but there are descents as well as ascents. In the distance you see snow-covered peaks glistening in brilliant sunlight. Your longing to reach those peaks is good, but you must not take shortcuts."[1]

Jesus, I understand glorifying You as trusting Your Life to be lived through me in every area, in every way and all with purpose. I am convinced I will not understand all that is happening to me. There are a million "Why's", but I am going to trust Habakkuk 3:19 today. I believe You are my invincible army! I **Invite You In** to speak to me through the Truth of these verses, Holy Spirit, even if I cannot see any fruit.

As I **Invite You In**, I desire a personal touch for my circumstance and relationships through this most difficult time.

> Habakkuk 3:19 - The Lord God is my Strength, my personal bravery, and my invincible army; He makes my feet like hinds' feet and will make me to walk [not to stand still in terror, but to walk] and make [spiritual] progress upon my high places [of trouble, suffering, or responsibility]!

79

JESUS IN THE STRUGGLE

Lord, I am certain You understand that when I am immersed in struggle, long illness, pain, suffering and grief, I want out, NOW! The results of more tests are coming. Am I being short-sighted again to Your eternal purposes? Must I always have to push through doubt and fear to arrive at some semblance of peace? Why am I consumed with those two enemies? Is the answer simply that this cancer of my soul and body is going to be victorious? Am I completely doubting Your trustworthiness and goodness? I **Invite You In** to minister to me in these dark places.

As I **Invite You In,** You bring Psalm 103 to me and what the Truth of Your perfect love means. Thank You, Personal, Loving God. I will feast on that today.

> Psalms 103:3 - Who forgives [every one of] all your iniquities, Who heals [each one of] all your diseases,
>
> Psalms 103:5 - Who satisfies your mouth [your necessity and desire at your personal age and situation] with good so that your youth, renewed, is like the eagle's [strong, overcoming, soaring]!
>
> 1 John 4:18a - There is no fear in love [dread does not exist], but full-grown (complete, perfect) love turns fear out of doors and expels every trace of terror!

80

JESUS IN THE DOUBTS

Jesus, is my love for You based on Who You are or what You do? That doubt enters by a portal based on a past misconception that You are not trustworthy. At this moment, I feel very disconnected from You because I am reverting to that deceptive filter which colors the manifestation of my physical healing (or my circumstance, whatever that may be). This must end! I desire Your "turning, changing and transforming all of my bed of illness." (Psalm 41:3) I do not see that change and it leaves me disappointed and discouraged. Instead, I cry out to You to turn, change and transform my focus where I see You face to face, regardless of my circumstance. I **Invite You In** to my weakness.

Author Sarah Young encourages me with, "Weakness and wounds are the openings where the Light of the knowledge of Your Glory shines forth."[1]

I sing with wonder, "What treasure waits within your scars?"[2]

As I **Invite You In**, You minister to those wounded places that I believe existed long before this illness with Your Presence.

> Isaiah 30:20 - And though the Lord gives you the bread of adversity and the water of affliction, yet your Teacher will not hide Himself any more, but your eyes will constantly behold your Teacher.

81

JESUS IN THE DARKNESS

Pastor Jack Hayford states, "Dark times are intended for your rest. When they come, lean back and recline in the everlasting arms of God."[1] I need deliverance or brain surgery to escape from my personal darkness.   This pit makes me believe that my feelings are my new reality. These need to be purged.   Jesus, my emotions are swirling and swirling because today I am so sick I cannot focus on You, on Truth. I **Invite You In** to extend Your righteous right hand to pull me from the mire. I know the only thing that will deliver me and do the necessary heart to mind transformation is Truth.

As I **Invite You In,** I see You reaching for me. What a beautiful, welcome sight!

> Psalms 40:2 - He drew me up out of a horrible pit [a pit of tumult and of destruction], out of the miry clay (froth and slime), and set my feet upon a rock, steadying my steps and establishing my goings.

> Isaiah 41:10 – 'Do not fear, for I am with you; Do not anxiously look about you, for I am your God. I will strengthen you, surely I will help you, Surely I will uphold you with My righteous right hand.'

> 1 Chronicles 16:11 - Seek the Lord and His strength; yearn for and seek His face and to be in His presence continually!

82

JESUS IN THE TIMING

I listened to Pastor Andy Stanley today. He asked a question I can certainly relate to: "Why doesn't God do something about 'that'?"[1] At every turn, I know God knows what my 'that' is. I listened carefully to the answer! Pastor said, "He can, because He is able."[2] Sometimes He waits (that ole timing thing, you know), but His timing is always perfect. Pastor Stanley was persistent in presenting the fact that we can trust Him in the meantime. Of course, it is because we can trust in promises He has made to us. He wants us to believe, to begin with. This should be followed by hope, trust and focus amidst the 'that'. I am glad he brought up the fact that sometimes living for God's glory and our good is not emotionally satisfying. Rather, this is what He has given us to hang on to when He seems inattentive.

At this moment, I receive Your promises, Jesus, as I must look to Who you are and Whose I am in the middle of my 'that'. I lean into Your grace because I know it is sufficient. I am seeking Your glory. I **Invite You In** to reveal that in my life and I know I will not be disappointed.

As I **Invite You In,** You restore my focus. I can believe and hope because of Who You are.

> John 11:40 - Jesus said to her, "Did I not say to you that if you believe, you will see the glory of God?" (NASB)

83

JESUS IN THE PLAN

Suffering. What a dreaded word. I know that by receiving Jesus as my Savior, Lord and Life, I signed up for the suffering program. Why suffering? What good can come from it? Is there some other way? Jesus asked the same suffering questions!

Jack Hayford, in *Free From Suffering*, relates that perfecting us is a by-product of Christ's sufferings. He, then, is our great example. Jesus submitted to a lifetime of the same kind of suffering that He knew we would have to experience. We think and reason in opposite ways from God. We often do not comprehend that God's ways are the very means of setting us free from the oppressive power of suffering.

Jesus, I **Invite You In** to work that in me! It is my desire to grasp this fully!

As I **Invite You In**, I am amazed at You and Your work and what You suffered for me.

> Luke 22:42 - Saying, Father, if You are willing, remove this cup from Me; yet not My will, but [always] Yours be done.

> Hebrews 2:10 - For it was fitting for Him, for whom are all things, and through whom are all things, in bringing many sons to glory, to perfect the author of their salvation through sufferings. (NASB)

84

JESUS IN THE DOUBTS

I am reminded today in Your Word, God, that in Christ I lack no good thing. The apostle Paul states in the New Covenant that all needful things are laid up for us in Christ. I know through Your endless, boundless wisdom every way and everything is perfect. That, alone, makes You worthy of my trust. This long illness eats away at my mind, will and emotions. Consequently, the truth that I lack no good thing feels false, even empty. For example, it is simply very difficult to breathe today. Lord, I desire for You to make Your promises tangible in my experience. I **Invite You In** to do just that.

As **I Invite You In**, it is just You and me. My decision is to believe You or not. I believe! Please line up my feelings with that, as You tend to any doubt.

> John 6:28-29 - Therefore they said to Him, "What shall we do, so that we may work the works of God?" Jesus answered and said to them, "This is the work of God, that you believe in Him whom He has sent."

> 1 Corinthians 14:1 - Go after a life of love as if your life depended on it--because it does. Give yourselves to the gifts God gives you...(MSG)

85

JESUS IN THE TIMING

Author Stasi Eldredge poses an often-asked question, "Is there a way to speed up the process of unveiling and hasten the change we are looking for?"[1] She must be reading my mail! As I walk in this illness (circumstance) day after day, month after month, which seems like forever when not feeling well, I know I must surrender all to You, Lord. This includes my thoughts and temptations of unbelief when I judge You as faithful and trustworthy or not, according to the circumstances of the day. How unfair it seems that I must Yield to what appears to be such cruelty from my Heavenly Father. Some days I am too ill to remember Your goodness, fearing the cancer of my soul more than the cancer of my body. Thank you! Thank you that You know my heart! No matter what my emotions want to tell me or my mind acquiesces to, You know my heart. My heart is new and transformed; it is a good heart. I yield and receive what You have for me, Lord, as slow as the process of healing seems. Today, I just **Invite You In.** I just need my Daddy.

As I **Invite You In**, I am reminded of Who You are, no matter what!

> Luke 7:23 - And blessed (happy— with life-joy and satisfaction in God's favor and salvation, apart from outward conditions—and to be envied) is he who takes no offense in Me and who is not hurt or resentful or annoyed or repelled or made to stumble [whatever may occur].

86

JESUS IN THE STRUGGLE

Pastor Charles Spurgeon informs us, maybe through his personal experiences, that we would not know some of God's graces if it were not for trials. He describes the trial experience as "afflictions", "black foils"[1] where God sets our jewels (graces) to make them shine. I believe I am in the midst of a good shining!

Jesus, I recognize that just as much as healing me physically is possible, You desire for me to turn full measure to You and trust You for the healing of my soul (mind, will and emotions). I am lying down beside still waters. Here you promise to heal my soul. As a result, I **Invite You In** today to aright anything in my thinking, that ole' battlefield of the mind, that would try to separate us; then, when the feelings attempt to drown me, I will know and know and know that I can trust You.

(Let this be a personal time of letting God speak to you about what is going on in your mind today to disappoint, discourage and depress you. You have the mind of Christ and He can stand you back up, Oak of Righteousness! **Invite Him In!**)

As I **Invite You In** I return to the familiar that I love so much, Your Life-giving Words.

> Psalms 73:25 - Whom have I in heaven but You? And I have no delight or desire on earth besides You. (NASB)

87

JESUS IN THE GRIEF

Author Anabel Gillam is one of my heroines of the faith. Gone to be with Jesus, she left us with so much richness in Truth and Love. She was desperately in love with Jesus, so much so that she allowed Him to lead her through the valley of the shadow of death in her own soul. The love union with Jesus spilled over into her marriage, the loss of her beloved son…oh, every area of her life. I miss her tiny frame and the few God-moments I had with her. I always wanted more. Today, one of her quotes stands out to me. She stated, "My emotions have difficulty thinking!"[1] I love that!

Oh Lord, as I cry out to You today, I cannot even think Truth. My emotions are swirling endlessly and I feel that I am caught in some vortex yanking me down, down, down. I **Invite You In** to rescue me with Your Truth and Your Way.

As I **Invite You In**, You lead and deliver me.

> Hebrews 11:1 - NOW FAITH is the assurance (the confirmation, the title deed) of the things [we] hope for, being the proof of things [we] do not see and the conviction of their reality [faith perceiving as real fact what is not revealed to the senses].

> 2 Corinthians 5:7 - for we walk by faith, not by sight-- (NASB)

88

Jesus in the Plan

I can certainly relate to Naaman in II Kings 5. Naaman was a sick man, the dreaded leper who would be shunned by all and sent out to live completely isolated, if he was not healed. So, he went to the healer of the day, Elisha. Elisha politely sends out a messenger to tell Naaman to go and dunk himself in the Jordan seven times and he would be healed. I thought the instructions simple. I also thought if I was him, I would do just as he was told by the man of God! But, no, Naaman became furious about the way he was to be healed, the particular river, and the fact that Elisha instructed him through the messenger. Naaman wanted Elisha to come out and wave his hand over him and poof, healing! Well, I am responding just like him. I am a Naaman.

Jesus, I have also come to You to be healed. Like Naaman, I have my own thoughts of how that should be accomplished. Because my healing is not happening the way I think it should, I add anger to the mix! I **invite You In** as I thank You that Your will and Your Way is perfect and You will work that in me. You are more than able to do for me what I cannot do for myself and You are accepting of my anger, too!

Lord, You spoke to me through Pastor Kenneth Copland who stated, "I quit looking for feelings and spectacular manifestations and just started to expect God to keep His Word."[1]

As I **Invite You In**, I ask You to escort me to the Jordan. I need to jump in seven times!

2 Kings 5:10-11 - Elisha sent a messenger to him, saying, "Go and wash in the Jordan seven times, and your flesh will be restored to you and you will be clean." But Naaman was furious and went away and said, "Behold, I thought, `He will surely come out to me and stand and call on the name of the LORD his God, and wave his hand over the place and cure the leper.' (NASB)

Psalms 119:160 - The sum of Your word is truth, And every one of Your righteous ordinances is everlasting. (NASB)

John 17:17 - Sanctify them in the truth; Your word is truth. (NASB)

2 Kings 5:13-14 - And his servants came near and said to him, "My father, if the prophet had bid you to do some great thing, would you not have done it? How much rather, then, when he says to you, Wash and be clean?" Then he went down and dipped himself seven times in the Jordan, as the man of God had said, and his flesh was restored like that of a little child, and he was clean. (NASB)

89

JESUS IN THE TURMOIL

Along my journey, I have learned that faith is deeply rooted in the heart and permeates the mind. It certainly is not discovered through emotions. Currently, if I believed what my emotions were telling me, I would be devastated. My dear sister in the Lord, Anabel Gillam states, "My only hope of meeting each circumstance in my life with stability and serenity and wisdom is to allow Him to meet each circumstance through me."[1]

Lord, I know this in my spirit. I have experienced this. Bring Life to that Truth again today because my emotions are powerful and desire to rule the day! I **Invite You In.**

As I **Invite You In**, You remind me of the very Truth that sets me free from my emotions.

> Psalm 16:8 - I have set the LORD continually before me; Because He is at my right hand, I will not be shaken. (NASB)

> Psalms 66:16-20 - All believers, come here and listen, let me tell you what God did for me. I called out to him with my mouth, my tongue shaped the sounds of music. If I had been cozy with evil, the Lord would never have listened. But he most surely did listen; he came on the double when he heard my prayer. Blessed be God: he didn't turn a deaf ear, he stayed with me, loyal in his love. (MSG)

90

JESUS IN THE WEAKNESS

Jesus, today, I simply must believe and receive Your Living Word. I have no energy to do otherwise if I want to survive the day. I **Invite You In.**

As I **Invite You In**, You desire to display Your faithfulness; You want me to be consumed by Your Love. You are even showing me today that just by thinking about You, I am praising You! You continue to show me You are faithful in having people pray for me, send me cards and emails, and do special things for me, as You live in and through them. I am so grateful.

> Hebrews 4:12 - For the Word that God speaks is alive and full of power [making it active, operative, energizing, and effective]...

> Psalms 103:1-5 - BLESS (affectionately, gratefully praise) the Lord, O my soul; and all that is [deepest] within me...forget not [one of] all His benefits--Who forgives [every one of] all your iniquities, Who heals [each one of] all your diseases, Who redeems your life from the pit and corruption, Who beautifies, dignifies, and crowns you with loving-kindness and tender mercy; Who satisfies your mouth [your necessity and desire at your personal age and situation] with good so that your youth, renewed, is like the eagle's [strong, overcoming, soaring]!

91

JESUS IN THE QUANDARY

During this lengthy recovery period, I've been given a great deal of time to ponder Truths from Your Word, Lord. For example, Abraham was ordered to sacrifice Isaac, yet Samuel was told that obedience was better than sacrifice. The juxtaposition of these two opposites puzzles me and I wonder if I can apply this confusion to my own life. You have given me a choice to trust You, Jesus, with this illness or default to fear. You do not need anything from me nor did You need anything from Abraham or Samuel. In both cases, could it be that through trust You want to remove fear, not create it? I **Invite You In** to minister to that place in me that stubbornly clings to anxiety!

As I **Invite You In**, You remind me that You really long to bring Life to all the hurtful ways within me; You really do have my best interest at heart.

> Deuteronomy 31:8 - It is the Lord Who goes before you; He will [march] with you; He will not fail you or let you go or forsake you; [let there be no cowardice or flinching, but] fear not, neither become broken [in spirit--depressed, dismayed, and unnerved with alarm].

> Psalm 112:6-7 – For he will never be shaken; the righteous will be remembered forever. He will not fear evil tidings; his heart is steadfast, trusting in the Lord. (NASB)

92

JESUS IN THE DECEPTION

What are we doing here, Lord? Am I believing the lie that I am missing a lesson(s) that I am supposed to learn? I know You are not a "teaching God". I don't have to learn a lesson before we move on. This mistruth has been taught over and over in my life, but I do not find it accurate, according to the New Covenant. Your goal is not to teach us but to have an intimate relationship with us. Consequently, New Covenant Truths of knowing You intimately as Life must apply here. That is the only place I can settle, because I am too tired to learn anything, too sick to get up and accomplish anything. All I can "do" is rest and abide. That just must be enough. I give you the ashes of my sickness, my mourning, my heavy, burdened failing mind and emotions. I **Invite You In** to exchange all of that. What is my present today?

As I **Invite You In**, You reveal to me the mission of Christ and the exchanges He has accomplished by way of the cross. I am certainly a recipient! Amazing!

> Isaiah 61:3 - To grant those who mourn...giving a garland instead of ashes...gladness instead of mourning...praise instead of fainting...(NASB)

93

JESUS IN THE FEAR

Fear has attempted to kidnap me again today. It is a fear that resembles wearing a permanent yoke around my neck. I fear never feeling better again, circumstances never changing, missing my grandchildren grow up and a host of other phobias. I know that when I pray with others in seeking the Lord for healing, once we pray for a yoke to be broken (given to Jesus), it is broken once and for all.

Lord, whatever I give You, You take it and You are not giving it back! Today, I pray in Jesus' name for the yoke of fear to be broken off me. I trust that is accomplished. I am certain that my feelings might lie to me even in the next few seconds, but I stand tall and firm in this moment! I believe the Truth that when You crucified my old man with its sinful nature and gave me Your Nature, You also took all the fear associated with that old man. You are Truth, Jesus! I **Invite You In.**

As I **Invite You In**, I bow for You to take the yoke of fear off me and give me Your light, burden-free yoke!

> Matthew 11:29-30 - Take My yoke upon you and learn from Me, for I am gentle and humble in heart, and you will find rest for your souls. For My yoke is easy and My burden is light. (NASB)

94

JESUS IN THE LOSS

God, if there is one thing I understand, it is that You have allowed this long illness. Somehow, some way, I must believe You will use cancer for my good. Pastor and theologian, Charles Spurgeon, spoke often about afflictions, how we should bless You for the losses that might become our security. So, here it is! I am face to face with surrendering my health and energy to You to use for Your glory. I am in union with You, so it is Your life being lived through me. This is kind of the 'in sickness and in health' Truth which brings exhilaration to my life revealing that You are with me in my nightmare struggles, every stinking moment of them. I know Your heart for me is to keep my eyes on You. You authored my life and You will finish it. It is comforting to know that You are running the race with me, and I pray that in the coming days, I will be more like Biblical Job, able to see You with my spiritual eye. I do not wish to just hear about You, I long to see You. I **Invite You In** to this difficult chapter in my life to minister to my heart as my Security.

As I **Invite You In**, I wait with bated breath to experience You, my only comfort today.

> Nahum 1:7 - The Lord is good, a Strength and Stronghold in the day of trouble; He knows (recognizes, has knowledge of, and understands) those who take refuge and trust in Him.

95

JESUS IN THE UNCERTAINTY

I am thankful that I still have joyful visions of what may lie ahead: preparing plentiful meals for my family, going for a long walk in the mountains, playing with my grandchildren, being with my friends for a movie and dinner. I am seeking to embrace what You have for me, Jesus. What is Your vision for me today, Lord? I **Invite You In** to speak to me about this during this long, tiresome journey.

As I **Invite You In**, I am astounded at what You say to me! I will hold fast to this, no matter what!

> Habakkuk 2:3 - For the vision is yet for an appointed time and it hastens to the end [fulfillment]; it will not deceive or disappoint. Though it tarry, wait [earnestly] for it, because it will surely come; it will not be behindhand on its appointed day.

> Romans 11:29 - For God's gifts and His call are irrevocable. [He never withdraws them when once they are given, and He does not change His mind about those to whom He gives His grace or to whom He sends His call.]

96

JESUS IN THE DOUBTS

I really believe that anyone who suffers for a lengthy period must ask questions from time to time. Today mine is, "How does this glorify You, God?" If I survive, always a looming question, what are the possibilities of bringing You glory? Hopefully giving You the glory for the healing is obvious. More difficult is the day to day, ins and outs of trusting You as my Rock when my feelings and eyes on circumstance cause me to waver in thought and emotions. If I simply rest and abide in You instead of considering this journey as labor, is that what You want me to grasp? Yes! My total dependence on Christ brings You glory!

Another epiphany! It is truly amazing that in my current state, I forget to come to You, Lord. I even allow my feelings to rule the day. For example, I am too frequently angry with You for allowing this illness; I feel depleted, both physically and emotionally, resulting in depression; I am unable to partake in my normal routine; etc. You ordained all of this so I could bring You glory by simply believing, trusting and abiding in You. I can just be me. I **Invite You In**, most precious Vine. I am drawn to abide!

As I **Invite You In,** You are clearing my vision to see what True Glory is – abiding with You!

John 11:4 - When Jesus received the message, He said, This sickness is not to end in death; but [on the contrary] it is to honor God and to promote His glory, that the Son of God may be glorified through (by) it.

Luke 6:8 - But He was aware all along of their thoughts, and He said to the man with the withered hand, Come and stand here in the midst. And he arose and stood there. 10 - Then He glanced around at them all and said to the man, stretch out your hand! And he did so, and his hand was fully restored like the other one.

1 John 4:17 - In this [union and communion with Him] love is brought to completion and attains perfection with us, that we may have confidence for the day of judgment [with assurance and boldness to face Him], because as He is, so are we in this world.
John 8:54 - Jesus answered, If I were to glorify Myself (magnify, praise, and honor Myself), I would have no real glory, for My glory would be nothing and worthless. [My honor must come to Me from My Father.] It is My Father Who glorifies Me [Who extols Me, magnifies, and praises Me], of Whom you say that He is your God.

John 15:1 - I AM the True Vine, and My Father is the Vinedresser.

John 15:9 - I have loved you just as the Father has loved Me; remain in My love [and do not doubt My love for you].

97

JESUS IN THE PURPOSE

Pastor Joseph Prince explains that God has a different view of healing the man with the withered hand than I do.[1] Jesus simply told the man to hold out his hand to be healed. Unfortunately, in most cases, I do not expect a miracle. God does not perceive Truth in the same realm we do. He uses the invisible realm of grace for healing and wholeness and therefore, miracles. His supply is superabundant!

I **Invite You In**, Jesus, and I desire to see as You do. I hunger to experience life with grace as I view my own personal withered hand.

As I **Invite You In**, I know I am seeking Your eyes for this situation and maybe a miracle, too!

> Mark 3:3 - And He said to the man who had the withered hand, Get up [and stand here] in the midst
>
> Mark 3:5 - And He glanced around at them with vexation and anger, grieved at the hardening of their hearts, and said to the man, Hold out your hand. He held it out, and his hand was [completely] restored.
>
> Ephesians 1:18 - I pray that the eyes of your heart may be enlightened, so that you will know what is the hope of His calling, what are the riches of the glory of His inheritance in the saints, which He has called you, the riches of His glorious inheritance in the saints (God's people)...(NASB)

98

JESUS IN THE STRIFE

Right now, all I can see is me
My sickness, my pain, my daily strife
My turned around, backwards, upside down life
Is there better for me, if I entrust this to You?
If so, what are You going to do?
I **Invite You In** to smooth the rough
To be my Comforter, my Enough
RHB

As I **Invite You In,** You let me see You through the eyes
of King David.

> Psalms 57:1 - BE MERCIFUL and gracious to me, O
> God, be merciful and gracious to me, for my soul takes
> refuge and finds shelter and confidence in You; yes, in
> the shadow of Your wings will I take refuge and be
> confident until calamities and destructive storms are
> passed.

99

JESUS IN THE DOUBTS

A line from a TV program caught my attention one evening. It went something like this, "Faith must not be questioned, only lived."[1] This is true because faith's authentic heartbeat is love. Lord, I have always said that faith equals the faith of Jesus and that I have all the faith I need because I have You. I am not questioning my faith, so how can I question Your love? I **Invite You In** to minister to this earthquake of feelings rumbling in my soul. You are Love, even when I do not feel it.

As I **Invite You In**, I find You: Love, Comfort, Sight, Strength, and Stronghold.

> 1 John 4:8c - The one who does not love does not know God, for God is love. (NASB)

> Psalms 62:5 - My soul, wait only upon God and silently submit to Him; for my hope and expectation are from Him.

> Psalms 94:19 - In the multitude of my [anxious] thoughts within me, Your comforts cheer and delight my soul!

> Psalms 146:8 - The LORD opens the eyes of the blind; The LORD raises up those who are bowed down; The LORD loves the righteous [the upright in heart].

100

JESUS IN THE DOUBTS

Pastor Joseph Prince speaks about God's love in my devotional today and he encourages with the Truth that I do not need to worry about loving God. I just need to let Him love me.[1] The more I allow this, the more I will fall in love with Him. Yes! The message of the New Covenant—receiving! Jesus, I do love You and I want to be buried so much in Your love that I will never doubt it, no matter how I feel. I am beginning to understand how I judge You by my circumstances. I repent for believing lies and doubting You. I **Invite You In** so that I may receive Your love. I believe it is freely given, so freely I receive.

As I **Invite You In,** You open my eyes to how You impart love to me. You ordain so many people around the world to pray for me. You send family and friends to take care of me and make sure I get transported to doctor's appointments and treatments. You send meals and cards and concerned phone calls. Thank You for loving me and forgiving my places of doubt. Not only have You forgiven them, but You have filled and continue to fill these nooks and crannies with Your love, because You have filled them with Yourself.

> 1 Thessalonians 5:24 - Faithful is He Who is calling you [to Himself] and utterly trustworthy, and He will also do it [fulfill His call by hallowing and keeping you].

101

JESUS IN THE PLAN

I believe my finite mind cannot begin to comprehend the extraordinary plans You have in store for me, Jesus. I think, in my present state, that concept seems preposterous, but I am not going to deny what I sense. You have the Master Plan and I believe when You call me, I will be able to respond. Even on my sick bed, whether at home or in the hospital, I am answering Your call of yielding to the flow of Your life through me. I see this manifested in my fruit bearing: kindness, when frustration is taking over; gentleness, when I feel like screaming; love, when I feel so agitated; faithfulness, when I feel like quitting; joy, when I am in pain; self-control, when I feel as if I am unraveling. Is that the extraordinary plan? I see You call me to what You have already equipped me with, Your Spirit. I **Invite You In.** You are the Source of my fruit.

As I **Invite You In**, I see that my Holy Spirit fruit basket will never be empty!

> Ephesians 3:20 - Now to Him Who, by (in consequence of) the [action of His] power that is at work within us, is able to [carry out His purpose and] do superabundantly, far over and above all that we [dare] ask or think [infinitely beyond our highest prayers, desires, thoughts, hopes, or dreams] —

102

JESUS IN THE DOUBTS

If I do not focus on You, Lord Jesus, I will be devastated by the dis-ease of my mind. Because You have the Master Plan for me, You already know my entire story from beginning to end. It is very foolish of me not to trust You. What does it mean to focus on You? In my Theology 101 way of thinking, I need to do a whole lot of Truth-talking to myself. I have heard some say it is "preaching the gospel" to myself. The Bible explains what "abundant life" is. If there is one thing I have learned, the only true abundant Life is in You, Lord, not this world. More than ever, I know that. Righteous Right Hand, please lift the face of my weary soul to You today. I **Invite You In** to do just that. I need to be "preachin'" today and every day.

As I **Invite You In**, I still find that You are the very best Preacher!

> Jeremiah 29:11 - I know what I'm doing. I have it all planned out--plans to take care of you, not abandon you, plans to give you the future you hope for. (MSG)

> John 10:10 - The thief comes only in order to steal and kill and destroy. I came that they may have and enjoy life, and have it in abundance (to the full, till it over-flows).

103

JESUS IN THE TIMING

I have often questioned Your timing in my life, Lord. Questions arise because Your continuum often contradicts mine! We appear to have been on different pages frequently, Lord. In my flesh, I believe this trial has nothing to do with Your perfect timing. Yet, the truth is, Your every calling is impeccable, has purpose, is not wasted and is not premature. Jesus, You will not allow me to remain here (in this grief, this illness, on this earth, etc.) one millisecond longer than what You have designed. Yes, Your timing is perfect. I **Invite You In** to tell me all about it.

As I **Invite You In**, You lovingly describe Your timetable through the revelation of Your Word. I yield to Your calling and trust the good that will ensue. The good in Your economy will be the best for me.

> Isaiah 55:8 - "My thoughts are completely different from yours," says the LORD. "And my ways are far beyond anything you could imagine. (NLT)

> Psalms 31:15a - My times are in Your hands...

> Romans 11:29 - For God's gifts and His call are irrevocable. [He never withdraws them when once they are given, and He does not change His mind about those to whom He gives His grace or to whom He sends His call.]

104

Jesus in the Deception

If my concept of You reverts to the long-standing lie that You are not trustworthy God, then my thinking becomes twisted. Deformed soul-concepts will cause me to bite the fruit of sin just as Adam and Eve did in the garden. I find myself immersed in a critical time where I need to be nourished by Truth. I define Truth as You, Jesus. I see You as the exact representation of God.

I choose to focus solidly on Truth today. The urgency of this need arises because there is talk of planning a funeral today—mine! In considering my own death, I have come squarely face to face with You, Lord. Either I trust You or I do not. I **Invite You In** to minister Truth to me. I am in You and You are in me. What characteristic of Yours do I need manifested in our union today?

As I **Invite You In,** I realize I can call on You to be anyone I need: Father, Husband, Lover of my soul, Best Friend. The list goes on infinitely. Because of Your faithfulness, You are everything I need.

Kay Arthur teaches that God's character is imparted in His Names:

- 2 Samuel 5:20 - The Lord of Breaking Through, Baal-perazim
- Genesis 1:1 - The Creator, Elohim
- Genesis 14:20 – The Most High God, El Elyon
- Genesis 16:13 – The God Who Sees, El Roi

- Genesis 17:1-3 – The All Sufficient One, El Shaddai
- Genesis 15:2 – The Lord, Adonai
- Exodus 13:14 – The Self-Existent One, Jehovah
- Genesis 22:14 – The Lord Will Provide, Jehovah-Jireh
- Genesis 15:26 – The Lord Who Heals, Jehovah-rapha
- Exodus 17:15 – The Lord Is My Banner, Jehovah-nissi
- Exodus 31:13 – The Lord Sanctifies You, Jehovah-mekaddishkem
- Judges 6:24 – The Lord Is Peace, Jehovah-shalom
- Malachi 1:10, 14 – The Lord of Hosts, Jehovah-sabaoth
- Psalm 23:1 – The Lord My Shepherd – Jehovah-raah
- Jeremiah 23:6 – The Lord Our Righteousness, Jehovah-tsidkenu
- Ezekiel 48:35 – The Lord Is There, Jehovah-shammah
- Isaiah 54:5 - For your Maker is your Husband--the Lord of hosts is His name--and the Holy One of Israel is your Redeemer; the God of the whole earth He is called.[1]

Exodus 3:14a - And God said to Moses, I AM WHO I AM and WHAT I AM, and I WILL BE WHAT I WILL BE.

105

JESUS IN THE SEARCH

I have so much time to reflect that my brain hurts! God, I recognize that You left us instructions in Your Word for every problem, every circumstance in life. Thank you for bringing me to Life in You by way of the cross. I possess You spirit-to-Spirit anytime. Author, Ann Voskamp calls it, "God gives God"[1]! I know that Your whisperings warn, lead and guide me each day. Your Word is that light and lamp guiding the way. Knowing You as The Way who intimately guides me through every turn and corner explains my ability to survive some days. I conclude that You are The Way, even when I feel lost and bogged down in the emotional vortex that wants to suck the life out of me. I am never lost. I **Invite You In** to be my Companion and Guide. There is no other that sustains me like You.

As I **Invite You In**, I see the invitation throughout Your Word to follow You. Lord, lead The Way.

> Psalms 23:4b - I will fear or dread no evil, for You are with me; Your rod [to protect] and Your staff [to guide], they comfort me.

> Isaiah 58:11 - And the Lord shall guide you continually and satisfy you in drought and in dry places and make strong your bones. And you shall be like a watered garden and like a spring of water whose waters fail not.

106

JESUS IN THE WEAKNESS

What a revelation! I can move mountains. Tell the mountain to move and it will! I see that in my weakness it is really You, Jesus, in and through me that can carry me to the finish line of this long illness, my current mountain. Until the cross and resurrection, no one understood that You would be coming to live in and through us, remaining in union with us. Therefore, I now have Your nature, attributes and character; not deity, of course! That would be heresy. It is simply the understanding that all of You lives through all of me. I do not have the strength to push through the day alone, but I can in You. I do not have the patience in my flesh to trudge day after long day by myself, but You do, and so the list goes. I can return and fill in the blank at any time! You are my patience, You are my courage, You are my_____. **I can do because You have already done. I can be because You Are.** I **Invite You In** because You are my Enough today. You will provide whatever fruit I need to bear today.

As I **Invite You In**, I believe that You are closer than my next breath. Please, let's move this mountain!

> Matthew 17:20 - ... For truly I say to you, if you have faith [that is living] like a grain of mustard seed, you can say to this mountain, Move from here to yonder place, and it will move; and nothing will be impossible to you.

107

JESUS IN THE DECEPTION

Author Ann Voskamp takes an old practice and adds an interesting twist: she states that we better be sure we are present with God instead of practicing His Presence, because, "You can always have as much of God as you want.[1]" We are the ones who need to focus on "waking" to His Presence.

I could not agree more! I sit here day after day and I must know I can be in touch with You, Holy Spirit, at any moment. I am thankful that if I "go to the left or right", off the beaten Way, You will call me to return. You do not shout, "Hey you! Get back on track!" Instead, with that most intimate call of all times, You simply ask, "Where are you?" I know that You desire a relationship with me as You did with Adam and Eve. I hear Your still, comforting, precious voice calling me to Truth so that I will not choke on the lies I am tempted to believe because of my present condition. Two most common deceptions are that You do not care about me and You are allowing this state of my being to go on and on. I need You. I need Truth whispered in my ear. I **Invite You In.**

As I **Invite You In**, through the stillness of my thoughts, I hear that familiar voice calling me to Truth, reminding me of all that is in my heart.

Isaiah 30:21b – Whenever you wander left or right: "This is the right road. Walk down this road." (MSG)

108

JESUS IN THE CONFUSION

Amidst confusion, I constantly return to the Truth. God, the answers I seek are given by Your Spirit and they come to me in thought and, of course, Your Word, the Bible. The Word of God is intimately personal, so much so that I can insert my name into any verse. It is written just for me. I am going to continue this cherished way of relating to You as You minister to me, Holy Spirit, through Your Word. I **Invite You In** through Psalm 121.

As I **Invite You In,** I believe that you are My Promise Keeper.

> Psalm 121:1-8 - I WILL lift up my eyes to the hills [around *(the four walls I am in daily)* Jerusalem, to sacred Mount Zion and Mount Moriah]—From whence shall my help come? My help comes from the Lord, Who made heaven and earth. He will not allow your *(my)* foot to slip *or* to be moved; He Who keeps you *(me)* will not slumber. Behold, He who keeps Israel *(me)* will neither slumber nor sleep. The Lord is your *(my)* keeper; the Lord is your *(my)* shade on your *(my)* right hand [the side not carrying a shield]. The sun shall not smite you *(me)* by day, nor the moon by night. The Lord will keep you *(me)* from all evil; He will keep your *(my)* life. The Lord will keep your (my) going out and your (my) coming in from this time forth and forevermore. (Italics mine)

109

JESUS IN THE PAIN

At this stage of the game, Jesus I need Your gracious responses more than ever. Without turning to You in the moment, I have negative, bitter, careless thoughts that can easily manifest in untrue, biting words. I do not want to be that kind of influence to those around me. If I look for Your grace by sight, according to my expectations, I will not be a witness of Your love or care for me. If I do not sit at Your feet continually, then I know that I cannot experience the unseen world of the Spirit from which You desire me to live. I must seek Your face, wait on You and bow to Your Way by faith. Do I believe this to be how I should live only when I am in a state of suffering? What I do believe is You are powerfully breaking down barriers to reveal to me that under any circumstance, I need You desperately. If the pain of this grief draws me this deeply to You, then so be it. I **Invite You In** to this bottomless place of need. I cannot even define it, but You can.

As I **Invite You In**, I come to the ever-present reality that You are closer than my next breath and You want to fellowship with me and minister to me. Break through, Lord!

> Hebrews 12:15 – Be careful that none of you fails to respond to the grace of God for if he does there can spring up in him a bitter spirit which can poison the lives of many others. (Phillips)

110

JESUS IN THE WEARINESS

I must focus on Jesus and not be dependent on feelings today because a blood infection has now been added to the mix. Sarah Young shares Jesus' thoughts on this matter, "Do not be discouraged by the difficulty of keeping your focus on Me. I know that your heart's desire is to be aware of My Presence continually".[1]

Do I crave what You can DO for me, Jesus? Or do I crave YOU today? If I crave what You can DO for me, I am simply dependent on circumstances and my emotions to dictate the outcome. I am faced with a week in the hospital and it seems so daunting. Do I handle it with an emotional soul response? Or do I seek You with a heart yearning to receive all that You are to me? That seems like a senseless struggle, but that is my battle today. The answer seems obvious but considering what is ahead—more needles filled with drugs that I despise coursing through my veins, a week in the hospital, more unknown challenges—I am asking for answers as I experience doubts and questions. The feelings are overwhelming. I **Invite You In** to make sense of these tumultuous emotions. I know I have the beautiful mind of Christ. I need the gift of clarity. I'm very tired.

As I **Invite You In**, I desire to see through Your eyes.

Psalms 119:2 - Blessed are they who keep His testimonies, and who seek, inquire for and of Him and crave Him with the whole heart.

111

JESUS IN THE PAIN

I am not feelin' it today, as the saying goes. Simply put, I feel awful. The drugs in my system produce so many negative effects. I could go into details but that does not really help. It's just one of those days.

Jesus, I simply **Invite You In**. What do You want to say to me?

As I **Invite You In**, I find that You have coined just how I feel today in Your Word.

> Psalm 116:1-9 - I LOVE the Lord, because He has heard [and now hears] my voice and my supplications. Because He has inclined His ear to me, therefore will I call upon Him as long as I live. The cords *and* sorrows of death were around me, and the terrors of Sheol (the place of the dead) had laid hold of me; I suffered anguish and grief (trouble and sorrow). Then called I upon the name of the Lord: O Lord, I beseech You, save my life *and* deliver me! Gracious is the Lord, and [rigidly] righteous; yes, our God is merciful. The Lord preserves the simple; I was brought low, and He helped *and* saved me. Return to your rest, O my soul, for the Lord has dealt bountifully with you. For You have delivered my life from death, my eyes from tears, and my feet from stumbling *and* falling. I will walk before the Lord in the land of the living.

112

JESUS IN THE WEAKNESS

One of my favorite passages is found in Psalm 27. Verse 8 has the word "seek" in it. I'm discovering what that really means. A word study reveals that the Hebrew word for "seek" is "baqash" and the Greek word for "seek" is "zeteo". They both impart the meaning of urgency: to aim, beg, require, to seek with all your might with much stress, a deep driving, hungering desire that motivates you; yet, without any work or labor.

In this moment, I aim for, beg, require, hunger after You, Jesus, with all my might, with that deep yearning of my heart. Thankfully, I do not have to labor after You. I can just rest in You, spirit to Spirit, with no strength to do otherwise. I **Invite You In.**

As I **Invite You In**, I am reminded through familiar passages from King David and Jesus, that You just want me to believe and abide in and with You.

> Psalms 27:8 - You have said, Seek My face [inquire for and require My presence as your vital need]. My heart says to You, Your face (Your presence), Lord, will I seek, inquire for, and require [of necessity and on the authority of Your Word].

> Matthew 6:33 - But seek first His kingdom and His righteousness, and all these things will be added to you. (NASB)

113

JESUS IN THE LONELINESS

With plenty of time to abide with You, Lord, and meditate on the New Covenant that You made with Yourself, I have come to understand that as downtrodden and useless as I feel, You don't need my help. What You really desire, even in my long-term illness and grief, is simply to dwell with Me. Your heart for me is to know and believe that You are present. I know that as I believe in Your love for me, I will not doubt Your many promises. I **Invite You In** to vividly make that my experience.

As I **Invite You In**, I know I'm free to run into the throne room of Grace shouting, "Abba, Abba!"

> Ephesians 3:17 - May Christ through your faith [actually] dwell (settle down, abide, make His permanent home) in your hearts! May you be rooted deep in love and founded securely on love…

> Romans 8:15 - For [the Spirit which] you have now received [is] not a spirit of slavery to put you once more in bondage to fear, but you have received the Spirit of adoption [the Spirit producing son ship] in [the bliss of] which we cry, Abba (Father)! Father!

114

Jesus in the Weakness

God, I look at Your promises to me and they are embodied in Your Word and the gifts You have already lavished upon me. Today, therefore, I call upon You, the great Jehovah Rapha, my Healer. You have imparted resurrection power and authority not only for strength to fight this battle, but also for strength to become more intimately connected with You. You have given me weapons of warfare, armor to adorn so I will not be defeated. I can "put" You on today because feelings verses Truth are at war! I **Invite You In** to fight this battle for me. I believe. This is a matter- of- fact day, indeed!

As I **Invite You In**, You show Yourself faithful in Your Word.

> Philippians 3:10-11 - [For my determined purpose is] that I may know Him [that I may progressively become more deeply and intimately acquainted with Him, perceiving and recognizing and understanding the wonders of His Person more strongly and more clearly], and that I may in that same way come to know the power outflowing from His resurrection [which it exerts over believers], and that I may so share His sufferings as to be continually transformed [in spirit into His likeness even] to His death, [in the hope] That if possible I may attain to the [spiritual and moral] resurrection [that lifts me] out from among the dead [even while in the body].

115

JESUS IN THE WEAKNESS

Jesus, I frequently dwell upon a Truth I understand more intimately. This Truth expresses how You labor for me: accomplishing the refining work in me and fighting battles. All I need do is rest and be still. Your sweet desire for me, Lord, is to depend on You. The "normal" activities of dressing, washing/drying hair, washing clothes, meal planning and preparing render me exhausted and out of breath as I collapse in my favorite chair. This recovery is a slow, slow process. All I seemingly "do" is rest. However, the bigger question is, am I resting in You? You have won the battle for my spirit on the cross. It is finished, completed, and I am seated with You in the Heavenlies.

This earthly battle of the soul (mind, will, and emotions) is another story. I deeply and daily understand the fact that the direction of my mind and what I choose to set my mind on will dictate my emotions. I must choose Truth. I must believe. I must rest. I must be still. I **Invite You In** because You are Truth. Please work and fight Lord. I cannot.

As I **Invite You In**, I hear, "Peace! Be still! It's okay to rest!"

> Psalms 116:7 - Return to your rest, O my soul, for the
> Lord has dealt bountifully with you

116

JESUS IN THE DOUBTS

What a radical shift! You've got me where You want me, Lord! Miss Energizer Bunny is still down and out. I am unable to "do" much of anything. I know from the New Covenant that You have done all the work. I am not suggesting that You will come and dress me and prepare my meals. What I do understand is that You have completed me in Christ. Throughout this trial and suffering, You have offered revelation: on this earthly journey, I have the choice to believe that truly, the work is done. This seems confusing until I search for the Truth. The work of the cross finished us and brought us to God, the Father; therefore, You, the Son, are seated at the Father's right hand. The Holy Spirit is present, living in me to live out the Truth on this earth that I am complete in You. It has nothing to do with trials, temptations, suffering, cancer of the body and soul. It has everything to do with my choice of how to respond out of Your life amidst the traumas and tragedies of this journey. Do I choose flesh, my way or Spirit, Your way?

I **Invite You In** today to show me just how complete I am in You.

As I **Invite You In,** You faithfully remind me that all I experience comes with a choice of believing that You really are for me, not against me. I understand the depths of this even more now that I embrace the New Covenant work of Christ. You are not only before me, beside me, behind me,

You live in and through me. I am totally consumed by Your Love which draws me to rest and abide in You!

> John 6:28-29 - They then said, What are we to do, that we may [habitually] be working the works of God? [What are we to do to carry out what God requires?] Jesus replied, This is the work (service) that God asks of you: that you believe in the One Whom He has sent [that you cleave to, trust, rely on, and have faith in His Messenger].

> Colossians 1:28 - We proclaim Him, admonishing every man and teaching every man with all wisdom, so that we may present every man complete in Christ. (NASB)

> Colossians 2:10 - ...and in Him you have been made complete, and He is the head over all rule and authority... (NASB)

> John 14:17 - ...that is the Spirit of truth, whom the world cannot receive, because it does not see Him or know Him, but you know Him because He abides with you and will be in you.

> John 15:5 - I am the vine, you are the branches; he who abides in Me and I in him, he bears much fruit, for apart from Me you can do nothing. (NASB)

117

JESUS IN THE SUFFERING

Some people describe suffering, long trials and grief, as "hell." I do not really believe we have a clue about hell. We have been saved forever from any realization of what hell is or could be. Christ saved us from that eternally and His life saves us from experiencing anything akin to that here on earth.

I might be down and out, but praise You, Jesus, I know better than to equate my experience with hell. Thank You that Your Life joined with mine enables me to enjoy You as my Peace, my Joy, my Love, my All-in-All and my Enough today. Yes, I long to feel better, be my ole' self, full of energy, but I'm learning what true Life in You is all about. I **Invite You In** so we can just "BE" today.

As I **Invite You In**, I am amazed at all the fruit, Peace, Joy, Love and Completion You bring to bear when I just rest in You.

> Romans 5:10 - For if while we were enemies we were reconciled to God through the death of His Son, it is much more [certain], now that we are reconciled, that we shall be saved (daily delivered from sin's dominion) through His [resurrection] life.

> Ephesians 6:10 - In conclusion, be strong in the Lord [be empowered through your union with Him]; draw your strength from Him [that strength which His boundless might provides].

118

JESUS IN THE DOUBTS

I realize this seemingly endless journey has brought new clarity to the message: You, Christ, are my Life through the New Covenant because You have given me revelation knowledge of Yourself. I believe all my years of counseling and teaching bore fruit because I trusted You to live through me. May I confess, however, that sometimes this part of my journey has seemed as if You threw me over board from an ocean liner and said, "Not to worry, you will make it back to shore!" A bit dramatic, I know, but that has sometimes been my perception. However, I now know more deeply than ever that every hungry, thirsty, wounded place is just a desire for You, nothing else.

I read A. B. Simpson's description of how he looked for You in every place for: sanctification, blessings, even healing. What He was looking for was not in the "it", but only found in You, Jesus, the Christ.

> "'I wish to speak to you about Jesus, and Jesus only. I often hear people say, "I wish I could get hold of Divine Healing, but I cannot." Sometimes they say, "I have got it." If I ask them, "What have you got?" the answer is sometimes, "I have got the blessing", sometimes it is, "I have got the theory"; sometimes it is, "I have got the healing"; sometimes, "I have got the sanctification." But I thank God we have been taught that it is not the blessing, it is not the healing, it is not the sanctification, it is not the thing, it is not the it that you

want, but it is something better. It is "the Christ"; it is Himself.'"[1]

I **Invite You In** to experience Your having filled every need I have today with Yourself.

As I **Invite You In**, I am not disappointed.

> 2 Peter 1:3-4 - For His divine power has bestowed upon us all things that [are requisite and suited] to life and godliness, through the [full, personal] knowledge of Him Who called us by and to His own glory and excellence (virtue). By means of these He has bestowed on us His precious and exceedingly great promises, so that through them you may escape [by flight] from the moral decay (rottenness and corruption) that is in the world because of covetousness (lust and greed), and become sharers (partakers) of the divine nature.

119

Jesus in the Plan

I awakened full of hope today. Nearing the end of treatment presents a whole new thought process. I am in the cycle of feeling ill the week of treatment and feeling better the next. My sickness during treatment week is not as severe now, hopefully because the disease is being arrested. A new understanding is that mental dis-ease is just as damaging as physical disease.

What takes my mind quickly off the trials of the day is praising You, Jesus. What cripples me quickly is a focus on my feelings and circumstance. I **Invite You In** today to be my focus. Praising You steadies my gaze!

As I **Invite You In,** I find that there is a realization that we are together in this no matter what the end of treatment brings!

> Romans 5:3 - There's more to come: We continue to shout our praise even when we're hemmed in with troubles, because we know how troubles can develop passionate patience in us... (MSG)

> Colossians 3:2 - And set your minds and keep them set on what is above (the higher things), not on the things that are on the earth.

120

JESUS IN THE BATTLE

I enjoyed what I recently read by John Eldredge. "We seek wisdom because the trail is narrow and hard to find. It is a cruel thing to tell someone to follow their dreams without also warning them what hell will come against them.[1]" Amen to that! We are warned at the ministry (Grace Life International) to understand, but not be afraid of, the tactics of the enemy against us. The Evil One's mission is not slight or haphazard; it is to "kill, steal and destroy" us.

At my first Oncology appointment You whispered Psalm 41 in my ear, Holy Spirit, (particularly verse 3 where You said You would sustain me in my sick bed and restore me to health). I knew it was "GAME ON!" with the enemy. I was living my dream: spending awesome times with my grandchildren, traveling, teaching and counseling for the ministry, and making my home my own after my recent move back to my home town. I certainly did not see this challenge coming! Now, it's here! Even as I am nearing the end of treatment, I must believe that You will never leave me helpless without being my Savior, my armor and defense. Jesus, I **Invite You In** to show me who You are amidst this battle for my life. Even with my improvements, my doctor reminds me there are no guarantees.

As I **Invite You In**, I am amazed at how well I am prepared to fight this battle, any battle, because of my union with You. By the way, Jesus, You are my guarantee of Life!

John 10:10 - The thief comes only in order to steal and kill and destroy. I came that they may have and enjoy life, and have it in abundance (to the full, till it over-flows).

Psalms 59:1 - DELIVER ME from my enemies, O my God; defend and protect me from those who rise up against me. (NASB)

Psalms 5:11 - But let all those who take refuge and put their trust in You rejoice; let them ever sing and shout for joy, because You make a covering over them and defend them; let those also who love Your name be joyful in You and be in high spirits.

1 Timothy 4:10 - With a view to this we toil and strive, [yes and] suffer reproach, because we have [fixed our] hope on the living God, Who is the Savior (Preserver, Maintainer, Deliverer) of all men, especially of those who believe (trust in, rely on, and adhere to Him).

Ephesians 6:10 - In conclusion, be strong in the Lord [be empowered through your union with Him]; draw your strength from Him [that strength which His boundless might provide].

121

JESUS IN THE UNBELIEF

Jesus, how do I relate to the Cross of Christ daily amidst this illness? To begin with, thank You for forgiving my sin of unbelief—past, present, and future. I seem to be challenged daily with this. I am so grateful for Your body given to be in union, spirit to Spirit, with me. You are a constant Source of Life whereas my focus can be on You, not my sin. My suffering, pain, exhaustion, loneliness, and threat of death are exchanged daily for Your Wisdom, understanding, healing, faith, hope and love. Above all, Your Love is the greatest gift. As I relinquish my burdens to You, I **Invite You In** to give me my presents for the day—that great exchange You made possible at the cross!

As I **Invite You In,** You, my Shepherd, are faithful to remind me that, in Christ, I have been given everything I need.

> 1 Corinthians 13:13 - And so faith, hope, love abide [faith--conviction and belief respecting man's relation to God and divine things; hope--joyful and confident expectation of eternal salvation; love--true affection for God and man, growing out of God's love for and in us], these three; but the greatest of these is love.

122

JESUS IN THE UNBELIEF

My daughter, Jennifer, was my caretaker for a few months. Her friend was led in a vision by Jesus to visit and pray with me; she told another friend and after five hours of driving, they surprised us with a knock on the door. What a celebration! His vision was carried out: sweet young women kneeling at my feet, laying on hands and interceding on my behalf! Eternal healing came to light! I believe physical and soul-healing occurred. I was soothed and comforted beyond anything I could dare ask or imagine. I believe I witnessed a miracle of His love for both my daughter and myself that night. I am filled with courage to walk a little longer, a little stronger.

I **Invite You In**, Jesus, the Source and Center of my healing.

As I **Invite You In,** I cherish *the many who have come to pray, anoint, encourage. I count them a heavenly gift.

> Acts 2:17 - And it shall come to pass in the last days, says God, That I will pour out of My Spirit on all flesh; Your sons and your daughters shall prophesy, Your young men shall see visions, Your old men shall dream dreams.

*The many are referred to in the acknowledgements.

123

JESUS IN THE PAIN

As I understand it, my plight today is part of the Father's greater design. Somehow, I fit snugly into the suffering section! I believe I signed up for this program many years ago when I said, yes to follow Jesus. The topic of suffering in every form is often discussed in the Word. The apostle Paul is a perfect example of a man who endured intense pain with great courage and strength. All the while, he beheld a vision of greater life in the Lord Jesus while he wrote most of the New Testament from a prison cell. With the flesh beaten off his back, he knew and understood suffering.

Lord, I do not compare my trial with his, but at the same time, my pain is my pain. What the outcome will be does not seem to be the point. What really matters is my response to You amidst it all. I **Invite You In, Jesus,** just as Paul did, to be my Joy and patient endurance. I want to know You in an intimate way because everything else is loss. Rubbish!

As I **Invite You In.** Vision and Comfort are given because You are the same God who carried Paul through his suffering.

> Hebrews 13:8 - Jesus Christ (the Messiah) is [always] the same, yesterday, today, [yes] and forever (to the ages).

> Philippians 3:8 - Yes, furthermore, I count everything as loss compared to the possession of the priceless

privilege (the overwhelming preciousness, the surpassing worth, and supreme advantage) of knowing Christ Jesus my Lord and of progressively becoming more deeply and intimately acquainted with Him [of perceiving and recognizing and understanding Him more fully and clearly]. For His sake I have lost everything and consider it all to be mere rubbish (refuse, dregs), in order that I may win (gain) Christ (the Anointed One),

Romans 5:3 - Moreover [let us also be full of joy now!] let us exult and triumph in our troubles and rejoice in our sufferings, knowing that pressure and affliction and hardship produce patient and unswerving endurance.

Romans 8:18 - [But what of that?] For I consider that the sufferings of this present time (this present life) are not worth being compared with the glory that is about to be revealed to us and in us and for us and conferred on us!

Romans 8:35 - Who shall ever separate us from Christ's love? Shall suffering and affliction and tribulation? Or calamity and distress? Or persecution or hunger or destitution or peril or sword?

Romans 12:12 - Rejoice and exult in hope; be steadfast and patient in suffering and tribulation; be constant in prayer.

124

JESUS IN THE TRAUMA

As I seek Truth through my cancer journey, it seems I must enter a maze of confusing pathways. It is as if entry is only gained through the front door of emotions. I imagined all along that feelings would be shoved to the back door of the maze, but that has not been the case. Treatment has ended and I truly thought I would just snap back. Yes, I did! However, my "Truth" maze continues to be full of twists and turns, some of which lead to dead ends! Some of the dead ends include mental, emotional and physical destruction that must be overcome. Others include old doubts, fears and trust issues, and an ever-present brain fog that I cannot clear up. Additionally, I bump into the after-effects of trauma. I never thought long-term illness could affect a person the same as war does to a soldier, but I similarly deal with very little physical strength, no stamina and an inability to participate in daily life—all PTSD symptoms. As I seek passage through this maze, I am certain there will be more dead ends.

Jesus, I **Invite You In** to lead me through this quagmire as You become my way, my stay, my every day. I want to experience You and all Your blessings in the twisting and turning of my recovery.

As I **Invite You In**, I find that King David sought You, Lord, following many of His traumas. He honestly expressed his emotions before he could arrive at the Truth. Therefore, I know I can come and write my Psalm 13 to You!

Psalm 13 - To the Chief Musician. A Psalm of David. HOW LONG will You forget me, O Lord? Forever? How long will You hide Your face from me? How long must I lay up cares within me and have sorrow in my heart day after day? How long shall my enemy exalt himself over me? Consider and answer me, O Lord my God; lighten the eyes [of my faith to behold Your face in the pitch-like darkness], lest I sleep the sleep of death, Lest my enemy say, I have prevailed over him, *and* those that trouble me rejoice when I am shaken. But I have trusted, leaned on, *and* been confident in Your mercy *and* loving-kindness; my heart shall rejoice *and* be in high spirits in Your salvation. I will sing to the Lord, because He has dealt bountifully with me.

125

JESUS IN THE DISCONTENTMENT

I remind myself that I must seek Joy, not happiness. Joy! Happiness is "a state of well-being and contentment[1]". On the other hand, Joy is defined as "delight, exultation" and there it is, "triumph"[2]! For the Jesus believer, this word can usher us into a whole new realm. During this "process", my only delight and well-being, contentment and triumph has been in Jesus. It certainly was not in the circumstances! Therefore, I emerged from difficult days knowing that "this, too, shall pass!" Likewise, I claimed "this is not my home." I live in a fallen world where there are trials and tribulation and disease, especially dis-ease of the mind.

However, the one Truth that I hold onto is that circumstances do not equal life. You are Life, Jesus. Coming to grips with earthly life or death is thought-provoking because I realize the entire journey has been Life! What an incredible revelation! Got that one, Lord, and that is my personal triumph as I walk through these recovery days ahead. I **Invite You In** to continue to carry me and "do" these days for me.

As I **Invite You In,** You assure me that You, indeed, are my Joy! My contentment is in You. You have not ceased your tender care of me just because treatment is over and there are better days ahead!!! I'm almost ready for a party!

Nehemiah 8:10b - Do not be grieved, for the joy of the LORD is your strength." (NASB)

126

JESUS IN THE TIMING

I've been reminded lately that You, Jesus, are the only living God out of all the gods of all the religions. You are also the only God that gives Life, Your Life, to us. While members of other religions pursue their gods, You pursue and even run after us. As I reflect over the last several years, You were present every moment, even when I did not feel Your Presence. It is impossible at any moment in time for You to be absent when I am one with You! I know it is Your desire for me to experience this Truth continuously—simply by believing. My dependence on my feelings certainly makes that difficult, but I am grateful for the hindsight. Thank You for being present in good times and bad. While I have earthly breath, I can count on the revelation that You are the same and You hold all things together. I do dare believe I will live more and more in Truth rather than in dependence on my feelings.

I **Invite You In** as I continue to walk, rest and abide in You and in the plan You have for me. All I must seek is the next step and You even light the path for me!

As I **Invite You In,** You impart the Truth that sets me free to believe.

Colossians 1:17 - He is before all things, and in Him all things hold together. (NASB)

127

JESUS IN THE BATTLE

Ann Voskamp states, "Every flood of trouble remakes the to-pography of our souls— making us better or bitter."[1]

Better or bitter? This is a question I deal with day to day. I believe the answer is encompassed within my momentary focus. The latest scan reads "better" as I experience new victories in this cancer battle (no hypermetabolic activity!). All the glory goes to Jesus, my Healer! However, what does my soul (mind, will and emotions) say? I realize this is a battle fought in the mind! One of the current battles is the length of the illness. It has been traumatic because the treatment was grueling, leaving behind its own scars physiologically and emotionally. Consequently, there are long-term battles that erupt. This can lead to "bitter" if I am not careful to focus on Jesus.

Why can't I be content with "better"? I am not experiencing traumatic treatment any longer! Is it because I am often tempted to believe the lie, the negative about any given circumstance? In this case, I doubt whether this prognosis will last which leads me back to my age-old battle, God is not trustworthy. The emotions and body then respond to what I am tempted to believe. The key word here is tempted. I may be tempted to head straight to the lie that motivates my flesh, a lie that tells me I am defeated in the battle. However, Truth as my default button was established by the finished work of the cross. Truth, a spirit to Spirit focus, says better, yes, MUCH better! This is what I can depend on when I want to focus on the lie of the moment and live out of negative feelings.

Jesus, I **Invite You In.** I hunger to sit in Your lap. You fight the battle!

As I **Invite You In**, I know the Truth heals and sets me free.

> John 8:32 - And you will know the Truth, and the Truth will set you free.

> Exodus 14:14 - The Lord will fight for you, and you shall hold your peace and remain at rest.

> Romans 8:5 - For those who are according to the flesh and are controlled by its unholy desires set their minds on and pursue those things which gratify the flesh, but those who are according to the Spirit and are controlled by the desires of the Spirit set their minds on and seek those things which gratify the [Holy] Spirit.

> Romans 8:27 - And He Who searches the hearts of men knows what is in the mind of the [Holy] Spirit [what His intent is], because the Spirit intercedes and pleads [before God] in behalf of the saints according to and in harmony with God's will.

> Hebrews 4:16 - Therefore let us draw near with confidence to the throne of grace, so that we may receive mercy and find grace to help in time of need. (NASB)

128

JESUS IN THE DARKNESS

There is a glimmer of hope today! I am feeling stronger a bit more consistently. As I reflect on Scriptures that have meant so much to me during this journey, I see Life in them even more as the fog of disease and mental dis-ease lifts. Glory! Seems as if I have lived the Exodus 33 passages.

This hope followed a period of dark questioning. I know that I argued with You, Lord. I felt I had been abandoned by You. Because I am one with You, I know that is impossible. However, I did not want to continue unless I saw a manifestation of Your Presence. You allowed me to see Your glory passing by putting me "in the cleft of the rock", just like Moses. That was You! You were covering me, holding me when I couldn't even see You or did not sense Your Presence. I need You today as much as I did in the throes of treatment.

Glory definition - God's glory and majesty. Not only referring to His outward manifestation, but an indescribable glory that Christ had with the Father before the foundation of the world. (John 17:5 - And now, Father, glorify Me along with Yourself and restore Me to such majesty and honor in Your presence as I had with You before the world existed.) [1]

Author Ann Voskamp states, "Is that it? When it gets dark, it's only because God has tucked me in a cleft of the rock and covered me, protected, with His Hand?...Dark is the holiest ground, the glory passing by."[2]

I, like Moses, **Invite You In** to continue to reveal Your glory to me. Thank You for allowing hope in the darkness.

As I **Invite You In,** You are glad to do just that by opening my spirit eye, more and more, to see You! Glory!

> Exodus 33:18 - Then Moses said, "I pray You, show me Your glory!"

> Exodus 33:20-22 - But, He said, You cannot see My face, for no man shall see Me and live. And the Lord said, Behold, there is a place beside Me, and you shall stand upon the rock, And while My glory passes by, I will put you in a cleft of the rock and cover you with My hand until I have passed by.

> Romans 8:17-18 - And if we are [His] children, then we are [His] heirs also: heirs of God and fellow heirs with Christ [sharing His inheritance with Him]; only we must share His suffering if we are to share His glory. [But what of that?] For I consider that the sufferings of this present time (this present life) are not worth being compared with the glory that is about to be revealed to us and in us and for us and conferred on us!

129

JESUS IN THE PLAN

My mind is racing ahead with plans that my body cannot keep up with. Do I really want to revert to some of my old habits of doing and thinking before this long illness? I have big plans, but I don't think You need anything big, God. You are big enough! I can certainly hope and dream and plans can be big, but You are there to direct every step. You have taken big out of my plans the last few years. Now what is left? Truth is left. The Truth is when suffering came on the scene, it was a part of Your plan. Oh! I did not go quietly, acknowledging my God-given lot! I went kicking and screaming! Gratefully, I've come out a bit shinier and re-fined. This illness was Your plan - The Plan. I **Invite You In** to continue to reveal to me that tailor-made plan!

As I **Invite You In,** You assure me that all I have to know is the next step and You will even direct that!

> Proverbs 16:9 - A man's mind plans his way, but the Lord directs his steps and makes them sure.

> Proverbs 3:5-6 - Trust in the LORD with all your heart and do not lean on your own understanding. In all your ways acknowledge Him, and He will make your paths straight.

130

JESUS IN THE IDOLS

I believe it is possible for me to make an idol out of anything! An idol can be defined as something that characterizes a person or something a person gives "life" to. I acknowledged early on that my focus on healing, instead of You, Lord, had become an idol. My current idol seems to be planning what is next! Really? I'm so glad you love me unconditionally and You know just how to call me to Yourself and slow me down. That certainly requires Your intervention, Lord! I **Invite You In** to show me where my focus needs to be; certainly not on that old question, "What am I going to do?" That will lead me back to my way every time. Rather, "What are You going to do today through me?" I want to be immersed in Your Way!

As I **Invite You In**, I see the age old struggle of my way versus The Way—flesh versus Spirit. Lord, for today, and that's all I have, I choose You! I believe You have plans for us!

> Jonah 2:8 - Those who worship hollow gods, god-frauds, walk away from their only true love. (MSG)

> Romans 8:6 – Now the mind of the flesh [which is sense and reason without the Holy Spirit is death. But the mind set on the Spirit is life and [soul] peace [both now and forever].

131

JESUS IN THE BATTLE

Okay, I'm whining. I do not even want to engage in the flesh versus Spirit battle that is raging in my mind. In fact, I cannot! My physical body will not let me push past where I am. How frustrating! Jack Hayford pens, "Once that deep seated confidence possesses you, and the conviction of certain triumph grips your soul, you come to understand the meaning of the eternal word: 'the joy of the Lord is Your Strength'."[1]

Oh Lord, my strength is in You! How do You want to manifest that today? I **Invite You In** because I do not seem to possess any in the natural realm!

As I **Invite You In,** I want to snuggle with You and I trust that You are my Joy and therefore, my Strength.

> Galatians 5:22 - But the fruit of the [Holy] Spirit [the work which His presence within accomplishes] is…joy…

> Philippians 4:13 - I have strength for all things in Christ Who empowers me [I am ready for anything and equal to anything through Him Who infuses inner strength into me; I am self-sufficient in Christ's sufficiency].

132

Jesus in the Plan

You are good especially when I seem to be in harm's way, Lord. This has piercingly become evident to me because I believe Satan has always intended to harm me. You will use whatever he throws at me for my good. I cannot grasp this right now, but I must trust You or I will be completely defeated. I've often wondered if Satan came and asked You if he could sift me like wheat? I believe he had to because You are the same yesterday, today and forever. Both the books of Job and Luke explain that Satan must ask permission from God before he can afflict us. You and Your plans have not changed.

You are also good when I doubt that You are. Ann Voskamp states, "The secret to the abundant life: to believe that God is where you doubt He can be."[1] This entire disease and dis-ease of the mind has made me consider Your sovereignty. I answer the question that looms in just about everyone's mind, "Are You God and are You good?" I believe far too often I get the circumstance and You, Lord, mixed up and that causes me to doubt Your goodness. Has my cancer diagnosis been good? Hardly!!! The question is, are You going to use it for my good? I must believe that You will. I **Invite You In** to comfort me and assure me with the Truth that You are the same yesterday, today and forever and You, indeed, are not only good, but You will use this part of my journey for my good!

As I **Invite You In**, I am invited to simply believe You.

Genesis 50:20 - As for you, you meant evil against me, but God meant it for good in order to bring about this present result, to preserve many people alive.

Job 1:12 - And the Lord said to Satan (the adversary and the accuser), Behold, all that he has is in your power, only upon the man himself put not forth your hand. So Satan went forth from the presence of the Lord.

2 Corinthians 1:3 - Blessed be the God and Father of our Lord Jesus Christ, the Father of sympathy (pity and mercy) and the God [Who is the Source] of every comfort (consolation and encouragement)...

2 Corinthians 1:5 - For just as Christ's [own] sufferings fall to our lot [as they overflow upon His disciples, and we share and experience them] abundantly, so through Christ's comfort (consolation and encouragement) is also [shared and experienced] abundantly by us.

133

JESUS IN THE WEARINESS

I feel as if I am attempting to climb up to my conductor's stand because I forgot to lead the choir to the final note. The choir continues singing and singing and singing. I can't seem to maneuver my way to the podium! Somebody please finish the piece, conduct the last note and we can all go home!

I rang the chemo bell! Did I think that was some magic moment that would end the effects of chemo, stress, tests and scans including years of follow-up? (Fill in the blank with your own trial.) The choir just keeps singing and singing the same chorale! I can't seem to stop it! My journey after chemo—did I really believe it was going to be "all over" without a care left in the world? Boy, was I naïve!

Most importantly, Lord, did I think I would not need to **Invite You In?** Did I believe I would be back to my old tricks of self-protection (flesh) which is my own way? That way of life did not work pre-cancer. In fact, that contributed to cancer of the soul (mind, will and emotions)! I **Invite You In** not as a "have to", but a "want to"! There is nothing that satisfies this weary soul more than to know that whatever I am in and whatever battle presents itself for the day, I need You!

As I **Invite You In,** there are no choirs that "sing" better, no sweeter songs than King David's Psalms!

Psalms 28:7 - The Lord is my Strength and my [impenetrable] Shield; my heart trusts in, relies on, and confidently leans on Him, and I am helped; therefore my heart greatly rejoices, and with my song will I praise Him.

Psalms 32:7 - You are a hiding place for me; You, Lord, preserve me from trouble, You surround me with songs and shouts of deliverance. Selah [pause, and calmly think of that]!

Psalms 42:4 - These things I [earnestly] remember and pour myself out within me: how I went slowly before the throng and led them in procession to the house of God [like a bandmaster before his band, timing the steps to the sound of music and the chant of song], with the voice of shouting and praise, a throng keeping festival.

Psalms 95:2 - Let us come before His presence with thanksgiving; let us make a joyful noise to Him with songs of praise!

134

Jesus in the Turmoil

This isn't fair! These temper tantrum words come marching through my brain like they have a right to be here! They take a stand as if I have a right to hold on to them. My emotions have a life of their own dictating the lies to be Truth. Truth, in man's economy, believes that life here isn't fair! Over time, I have learned to define life very differently. If I look at life and define it as circumstances, that can be gloomy business – not fair. But, if I look at Life as Christ, [after all, He is the Way, the Truth and the Life] my circumstances take on an entirely different appearance.

At this particular moment, suffering and grief, day after day, do not seem fair. Am I going to just go deeper inside myself with all of these emotions? Or, am I going to seek Your face, Jesus, the face of Life, and exchange my feelings for what it is You want me to have of Your Life? I **Invite You In** and please bring a dump truck because I'm getting ready to heap a load of emotions on You!

As I **Invite You In**, You welcome me; You love me; You even want these emotions so that You can exchange them for what You died for me to have in the moment. Thank you Lord. I'm coming to get my present!

> John 14:6 - Jesus said to him, "I am the [only] Way [to God] and the [real] Truth and the [real] Life; no one comes to the Father but through Me.

Psalms 27:8 - You have said, Seek My face [inquire for and require My presence as your vital need]. My heart says to You, Your face (Your presence), Lord, will I seek, inquire for, and require [of necessity and on the authority of Your Word].

Matthew 7:11 - If you then, evil as you are, know how to give good and advantageous gifts to your children, how much more will your Father Who is in heaven [perfect as He is] give good and advantageous things to those who keep on asking Him!

James 1:17 - Every good gift and every perfect (free, large, full) gift is from above; it comes down from the Father of all [that gives] light, in [the shining of] Whom there can be no variation [rising or setting] or shadow cast by His turning [as in an eclipse].

Isaiah 61:3 -To grant [consolation and joy] to those who mourn in Zion—to give them an ornament (a garland or diadem) of beauty instead of ashes, the oil of joy instead of mourning, the garment [expressive] of praise instead of a heavy, burdened, *and* failing spirit—that they may be called oaks of righteousness [lofty, strong, and magnificent, distinguished for uprightness, justice, and right standing with God], the planting of the Lord, that He may be glorified.

135

JESUS IN THE GRIEF

I am learning that the key to living a fulfilling life is to avoid getting stuck. Getting stuck in grief is like falling into miry clay. This sticky substance is like well-rehearsed, gloom-filled emotions. However, they only lead a person down to the depths of despair. There comes a point, a real deciding point of the will, to give less credence to feelings and above all, not to get stuck in them. Rather, we can come to the Father to let Him shed focus and light on emotions.

Where do all these negative emotions originate? What are they attached to? They must be attached to a deceptive thought! Feelings do not possess the quality of truth or deception; only thoughts do. Like King David, I do have power over what I think and believe.

Lord, David succeeded at pouring out his feelings to You and he could turn on a dime in his current circumstance and be right where he needed to be—in Your lap, a lap where Truth is found. I **Invite You In** to experience You today, because You are Truth.

As I **Invite You In**, I am never disappointed at our friendship, Lord. Like the best of friends, You listen, You do not judge; You walk with me and talk with me and give of Yourself to me in exchange for all the destructive feelings. The wonderful thing is that I can crawl in Your lap at any time! Thank You!

Psalm 13:1, 2, 5 - HOW LONG will You forget me, O Lord? Forever? How long will You hide Your face from me? How long must I lay up cares within me and have sorrow in my heart day after day? How long shall my enemy exalt himself over me? But I have trusted, leaned on, and been confident in Your mercy and loving-kindness; my heart shall rejoice and be in high spirits in Your salvation.

Psalms 40:2 - He brought me up out of a horrible pit [of tumult and of destruction], out of the miry clay, And He set my feet upon a rock, steadying my footsteps and establishing my path.

Psalms 94:19 - In the multitude of my [anxious] thoughts within me, Your comforts cheer and delight my soul!

Psalms 107:9 - For He satisfies the longing soul and fills the hungry soul with good.

Psalms 116:7 - Return to your rest, O my soul, for the Lord has dealt bountifully with you.

Psalms 143:6 - I spread forth my hands to You; my soul thirsts after You like a thirsty land [for water]. Selah [pause, and calmly think of that]!

136

JESUS IN THE SURRENDER

Lord, I am beginning to understand what life choices boil down to. The will. I can do; I can think; I can will, but in the end, I pray not my will but Your will be done. If You will to bring me through this deep grief process, this long illness, then Thy will be done!

The word "surrender" is difficult in terms of seeking Your will because it could intimate a loss. I choose the word 'yield' instead. I yield to Your will, Lord, because my will is going to want what I want when I want, the way I want, why I want and how I want. Frankly, I have no desire to suffer to get where I need to be. Like a meteor shooting straight down from heaven into my heart and exploding with Your love, Your goodness and Your mercy bestowed upon me is Your will. It's so difficult to see through happenings here on earth. Death, sickness, illness—You are here to guide us through the center of all struggles; not take us around, over, or under them, but through them—facing them head on. The prophet Isaiah explains this very clearly when speaking about the way You lead us through the sufferings of life. I believe You accomplish Your will in and through us for one purpose and one purpose only, to make us and mold us into the image of Jesus. I **Invite You In** to put me on the potter's wheel. I am but clay!

As I **Invite You In**, I cannot be excited about the suffering, but I can look forward to seeing just how Christ will manifest His life in and through me. Mold me, Lord!

Matthew 6:10 - Your kingdom come, Your will be done on earth as it is in heaven.

Isaiah 43:2 - When you pass through the waters, I will be with you, and through the rivers, they will not overwhelm you. When you walk through the fire, you will not be burned or scorched, nor will the flame kindle upon you.

Isaiah 64:8 - But now, O LORD, You are our Father, We are the clay, and You our potter; And all of us are the work of Your hand.

Jeremiah 18:6 - "Can I not, O house of Israel, deal with you as this potter does?" declares the LORD. "Behold, like the clay in the potter's hand, so are you in My hand, O house of Israel.

Romans 8:29 - For those whom He foreknew [of whom He was aware and loved beforehand], He also destined from the beginning [foreordaining them] to be molded into the image of His Son [and share inwardly His likeness], that He might become the firstborn among many brethren.

137

JESUS IN THE UNCERTAINTY

The only way I accomplish anything most days is to focus on You, Jesus. I know that should be the norm for every Christ believer, but personally, I must really focus on Your suffering. How did You manage Your agony? It is Your desire for me to understand, every single moment, that You do not see things as they appear, especially as sight applies to suffering.

Jack Hayford states, "Jesus has broken the ability of suffering to reduce us to bitterness or disobedience. He wants to fill us with the same life that brought Him through suffering that kept Him from growing weary in well doing."[1] *What is so amazing is that You have already filled me with Your life that I may not grow weary in doing well. You mean I can do well amidst this long period of grief and illness? I **Invite You In** today because I need Your eyes for all this.

As I **Invite You In**, I desire to put on Your glasses to view every situation.

> Galatians 6:9 - Let us not grow weary *or* become discouraged in doing good, for at the proper time we will reap, if we do not give in.

> Romans 8:18 - For I consider that the sufferings of this present time are not worthy to be compared with the glory that is to be revealed to us.

138

JESUS IN THE QUANDARY

Seemingly, I have fallen into the same trap that A.B Simpson, founder of Christian and Missionary Alliance, did over one hundred years ago! He was seeking healing: go here, pray with this person, take this remedy. There is validity in all that unless it becomes a means to what a person believes will heal. Then, seeking healing can take on an idol status. I have always loved Simpson's testimony where he discusses seeking Jesus. He did so in many arenas, including healing. He states, "And so I thought the healing would be an it, too, that the Lord would take me like the old run-down clock, wind me up, and set me going like a machine. It is not thus at all. I found it was Himself coming in instead and giving me what I needed at the moment."[1]

How easy it is to get caught up in that search. When I've suffered for a long time and then must wait, rest, abide, I begin to feel as if there are heavy rocks hanging around my neck. This heaviness creeps in because my focus shifts off Jesus. Mr. Simpson found the only remedy for these maladies: "I had to learn to take from Him my spiritual life every second, to breathe Himself in as I breathed, and breathe myself out. So, moment by moment for the spirit, and moment by moment for the body, we must receive".[2] Jesus is Truth. We are one with Him in union. With that combination, there is freedom in waiting, resting and abiding. Each becomes sweet, intimate times of expecting Jesus to just be God!

I have found what A B Simpson found is also my Enough – "At last He said to me - Oh so tenderly - "My child, just take Me, and let Me be in you the constant supply of all this, Myself." And when at last I got my eyes off my sanctification, and my experience of it, and just placed them on the Christ in me, I found, instead of an experience, the Christ larger than the moment's need, the Christ that had all that I should ever need who was given to me at once, and forever…" [3]

I receive that! I **Invite You In** Jesus.

As I **Invite You In,** You desire for me to realize the fullness of all that You are, especially now in my healing.

> Ephesians 3:19 - [That you may really come] to know [practically, through experience for yourselves] the love of Christ, which far surpasses mere knowledge [without experience]; that you may be filled [through all your being] unto all the fullness of God [may have the richest measure of the divine Presence, and become a body wholly filled and flooded with God Himself]!

> Colossians 2:2 - [For my concern is] that their hearts may be braced (comforted, cheered, and encouraged) as they are knit together in love, that they may come to have all the abounding wealth and blessings of assured conviction of understanding, and that they may become progressively more intimately acquainted with and may know more definitely and accurately and thoroughly that mystic secret of God, [which is] Christ (the Anointed One).

139

JESUS IN THE FEAR

I've been forced to take a good look at the emotion of fear. Why? Because I'm afraid! This is not an emotion that I am comfortable with, at all. What am I afraid of? The unknown of what is going to happen. Did I respond to treatment? How will this affect and change my life? What next? Will this grief ever end? Well, there is my list!

Malcolm Smith, Pastor and Founder of Unconditional Love Fellowship, states that if we go to the "what if's" and "if onlys" of life then God is not there. Why? Because He is the great I AM and He is only in the moment. I turn my focus on You, Jesus. All those questions lead me down a slippery, dark slope. The Truth is I don't need to know answers. This perceived need only feeds into my trying to control what is completely out of my control! There is no good end to that!

Jesus, I **Invite You In** to rein me back in, slow me down and place me where You are - in the moment.

As I **Invite You In**, You are more than willing to remind me of Who You are - for all of time, a moment by moment God. The great I AM.

> Exodus 3:14 - And God said to Moses, I AM WHO I AM and WHAT I AM, and I WILL BE WHAT I WILL BE; and He said, You shall say this to the Israelites: I AM has sent me to you!

140

Jesus in the Depression

Hope clears vision while disappointment is a stepping stone to discouragement. This leads to despair and BOOM, the box of depression appears! How can we overcome this dangerous path? Hope! Hope in what? Or better yet, hope in Whom? I find that if I just hope in my circumstances, i.e., feeling better, stronger, having no grief, seeing a little light in the tunnel, then I must wait on something to change.

If I know, believe and act on the fact that You, Jesus, are my Hope, then a major shift to my vision occurs. I bypass seeing my circumstance to seeing that You have my circumstance in Your hands! Hope is not rooted in what You are going to do with those circumstances. It is You alone, the Hope of glory. I find I need to rehearse that every day. I am preaching the gospel to myself today. I **Invite You In,** my Hope!

As I **Invite You In**, I am never disappointed in what You say and how You give sweet reminders of Your Truth.

> Matthew 12:21 - "AND IN HIS NAME THE GENTILES (all the nations of the world) WILL HOPE [with confidence]."

> Colossians 1:27 - to whom God willed to make known what is the riches of the glory of this mystery among the Gentiles, which is Christ in you, the Hope of glory.

141

JESUS IN THE IDOLS

Idols creep in and offer pathetic substitutes in our search to have our needs met for love, acceptance, worth and security. Much like going to a banquet feast and never going past the hors d'oeuvres table, we believe these morsels are all that are offered! Those tasty tidbits are a poor substitute for a lavish meal! Idols soothe the savage beast making one feel as if "all is well". During this long, long grief period, I've consumed many "tidbits" to try to get my needs met. Regretfully, occasional taste-testing has caused me to walk away from intimacy with my Jesus.

The Truth—Jesus, You never move away from me! That's impossible since we are in union—You in me and me in You. I tend to forget that! I know and believe this Truth but I currently seem to be experiencing spiritual amnesia. You are in me and because of that union, I can fill in the blank. As defined by You, I am_____(a child of God, righteous, Christ's friend, etc.) The list is endless. The flip-side of the union is that I am in You and because of that union, You are_____(Omnipotent, Father, Mother, spouse, Lover of my soul, Mighty God, etc.) This is an endless list. So, idols be gone! You can never meet my needs today. Lord, **I Invite You In.** I stand believing that You have everything I need in You. I won't settle for morsels any longer.

As I **Invite You In**, there is such a stark contrast in You, Jesus, vs idols, I wonder how I continue to fall for the lie that something or someone else can give me the depths of what I need. When I turn to idols I forfeit Your grace in the moment.

Jonah 2:8 - Those who pay regard to false, useless, and worthless idols forsake their own [Source of] mercy and loving-kindness.

Isaiah 27:9 - ...this shall be the full fruit [God requires] for taking away his sin: that [Israel] should make all the stones of the [idol] altars like chalk stones crushed to pieces...

1 John 5:21 - Little children, keep yourselves from idols (false gods)--[from anything and everything that would occupy the place in your heart due to God, from any sort of substitute for Him that would take first place in your life]. Amen (so let it be).

Romans 6:11 - Even so, consider yourselves to be dead to sin [and your relationship to it broken], but alive to God [in unbroken fellowship with Him] in Christ Jesus.

Romans 8:10-11 - But if Christ lives in you, [then although] your [natural] body is dead by reason of sin and guilt, the spirit is alive because of [the] righteousness [that He imputes to you]. And if the Spirit of Him Who raised up Jesus from the dead dwells in you, [then] He Who raised up Christ Jesus from the dead will also restore to life your mortal (short-lived, perishable) bodies through His Spirit Who dwells in you.

142

JESUS IN THE DECEPTION

I have never considered myself to be a hoarder. I see that practice can take on many facades, but I'm truly not a hoarder of things. In fact, I am just the opposite, I throw everything away and that can be a problem as well! I believe during the process of this illness, grief, misery, I've allowed negative thoughts, very purposeful negative thoughts to gather in the recesses of my mind. Consequently, I am a hoarder of thoughts packed nicely with feelings. They may appear harmless, even ornamental, but they can be deadly. I see that emotions can be a source of soul-hoarding when gathered and never given over to Truth. We easily accept the lie that feelings are attached to. They are certainly stealers of my Joy and Peace. I've learned that the fruit of The Spirit are not traits that are just going to naturally come to me, but are characteristics of the Source of Life—Jesus. Lest I forget, He lives in me! I can hoard all negative, no good, joy and peace-stealing thoughts complete with feelings until there is not one inch left for anything; or, I can sweep clean those lies by exchanging them for Truth, the gifts with which God desires for me to replace my stinking thinking. Truth comes in, lies and feelings go out as He cleans out the rooms of my mind and heart. I can collect, even hoard His thoughts with my mind of Christ.

I **Invite You In** to clean house, Jesus.

As I **Invite You In,** You are present to exchange all the deception for the Truth of Who You are and who You say that I am—a clean vessel!

1 Corinthians 2:16 - For who has known *or* understood the mind (the counsels and purposes) of the Lord so as to guide *and* instruct Him *and* give Him knowledge? But we have the mind of Christ (the Messiah) *and* do hold the thoughts (feelings and purposes) of His heart.

1 Corinthians 6:11 -... But you were washed clean (purified by a complete atonement for sin and made free from the guilt of sin), and you were consecrated (set apart, hallowed), and you were justified [pronounced righteous, by trusting] in the name of the Lord Jesus Christ and in the [Holy] Spirit of our God.

1 Corinthians 1:30 - But it is from Him that you have your life in Christ Jesus, Whom God made our Wisdom from God, [revealed to us a knowledge of the divine plan of salvation previously hidden, manifesting itself as] our Righteousness [thus making us upright and putting us in right standing with God], and our Consecration [making us pure and holy], and our Redemption [providing our ransom from eternal penalty for sin].

James 1:17 - Every good thing given and every perfect gift is from above, coming down from the Father of lights, with whom there is no variation or shifting shadow.

143

JESUS IN THE SEARCH

St. Augustine, a saint of the early church, pens, "...you have made us for Yourself and our hearts are restless until they find their rest in You."[1] I have never known that to be so vividly true until I experienced this long, drawn-out grief and illness. I am restless and I wonder if this is because I do not feel well; because I am so sad at watching what has happened to my health and vitality; because I'm not working at the ministry. I think all the above could be part of the answer. However, I must answer the question, no matter what, where is true joy found? How do I obtain what appears to be an elusive gift? Is it even possible to find this treasure when illness seems to have a strangle-hold? I must look at the Apostle Paul's life for answers. He teaches it is possible to find True Joy. I realize he has experienced heaven and has seen what I have not, but all the same, the Truth is The Jesus that lived in Paul on this earth lives in me. Furthermore, the fruit of the Spirit that is manifested in Paul is manifested in me. Consequently, one can assume correctly that some "thing" can block the flow of the Spirit.

You, Jesus, certainly do not withhold anything from me. Must it be my stinking thinking again? Does that mean I am a lie and a few feelings away from You? I **Invite You In** to reveal this to me Lord. Show me what I am choosing that holds me captive in my mind that would keep me away from Your lap!

As I **Invite You In,** You reveal to me that that **anything,** any thought that sets itself up against Who You say You are and who You say I am, can and will hinder the intimacy that I desire. I must give my thoughts the litmus test of Truth. Do my thoughts line up with Your thoughts?

> Nehemiah 8:10b - And be not grieved and depressed, for the joy of the Lord is your strength and stronghold.

> Isaiah 55:8-9 - "For My thoughts are not your thoughts, nor are your ways My ways," declares the LORD. "For as the heavens are higher than the earth, So are My ways higher than your ways And My thoughts than your thoughts."

> 2 Corinthians 10:5 - [Inasmuch as we] refute arguments and theories and reasonings and every proud and lofty thing that sets itself up against the [true] knowledge of God; and we lead every thought and purpose away captive into the obedience of Christ (the Messiah, the Anointed One)...

144

JESUS IN THE PAIN

I believe Jesus intends the Gospel to be a profound message of God's rescue through pain. Therein lies a very specific tension: Satan cannot touch me without first asking permission from You, Lord. As eluded to earlier, You instruct him as to the amount of physical harm he can do, just as You did concerning Job. There is no difference between Job's situation and mine! Why? Because You are in control of the circumstances of my suffering. Just like Job, I have a choice as to how I will respond. This is profound but I must **Invite You In** to gain understanding.

How do I overcome the notion that if You loved and cared for me You would not let me suffer? As the heroic Yoda might say, "Overcome this notion I must!" I yearn for You to rescue me through the pain. I **Invite You In** to do just that. I know You are the same God that rescued Job. I desire for my spiritual eye to see You.

As I **Invite You In**, You bring light to Your promises. I believe You will not break Your promises to me and I will intimately know You as I have never known You before!

Hebrews 13:8 - Jesus Christ (the Messiah) is [always] the same, yesterday, today, [yes] and forever (to the ages).

Job 1:12 - And the Lord said to Satan (the adversary and the accuser), Behold, all that he has is in your power; only upon the man himself put not forth your hand. So Satan went forth from the presence of the Lord.

Job 2:5-6 - But put forth Your hand now, and touch his bone and his flesh, and he will curse and renounce You to Your face. And the Lord said to Satan, Behold, he is in your hand; only spare his life.

Job 42:1-2 – Then Job said to the Lord, I know that You can do all things, and that no thought or purpose of Yours can be restrained or thwarted.

Job 42:5 - I had heard of You [only] by the hearing of the ear, but now my [spiritual] eye sees You.

Isaiah 43:2 - When you pass through the waters, I will be with you, and through the rivers, they will not overwhelm you. When you walk through the fire, you will not be burned or scorched, nor will the flame kindle upon you.

145

JESUS IN THE STRUGGLE

I seem to struggle with this question frequently: how can deception have so much power? The answer must be found in whether I believe it or not! God, the lie I am tempted to believe about You, on an emotional level, is You are untrustworthy. We have been through this many times before! That tosses me about like a wave, creating double-mindedness when I fall prey to it. It all goes back to Satan's work in the garden. He lied to Adam and Eve and they believed him. As a result, they hid from God. They disconnected from fellowship with You and believed that You were no longer pure, unconditional Love.

As a new creation, I know Who You are, but feelings want to take me back to my flesh and believe that circumstances are Who You are. Yes, Satan is alive and active while I am on this earth and no matter how I will myself to believe the Truth, so often emotions want to rule. They seem to bear Truth because of the weakness of my flesh. Somehow, judgment takes place and I am tempted to look at my circumstances and come into agreement with terrible deceptions. Will I ever be rid of the temptation to believe the lies because they shake me to my core?

I **Invite You In**. When I fall prey to the untruths, my spirit eye is covered from seeing You and all that You are to me. I am left feeling abandoned, alone, and afraid. What a horrible deceptive triangle!

As I **Invite You In**, I know if I can just stand in believing the Truth, You always win the battle because the enemy is already defeated. Therefore, my eyebeam, my focus when there is not a fiber of my being that feels it, will land squarely on You. You will deliver me from this place and I will be free of it!

> Genesis 3:8 - When they heard the sound of GOD strolling in the garden in the evening breeze, the Man and his Wife hid in the trees of the garden, hid from GOD. (MSG)

> James 1:6 - Only it must be in faith that he asks with no wavering (no hesitating, no doubting). For the one who wavers (hesitates, doubts) is like the billowing surge out at sea that is blown hither and thither and tossed by the wind.

> Psalms 20:1 - MAY THE Lord answer you in the day of trouble! May the name of the God of Jacob set you up on high [and defend you];

> Luke 18:3 - And there was a widow in that city who kept coming to him and saying, protect and defend and give me justice against my adversary.

> Luke 18:7 - And will not [our just] God defend and protect and avenge His elect (His chosen ones), who cry to Him day and night? Will He defer them and delay help on their behalf?

> John 8:31 - And you will know the Truth, and the Truth will set you free.

146

JESUS IN THE DECEPTION

The more I focus on Who Jesus is and whose I am, I see the enemy has no open door, no territory to run through my soul (mind, will and emotions) and wreak havoc. That, indeed, requires a watchful spirit eye! I choose to believe the Truth, because the lies want to march through like an enemy army according to my emotions in any given moment. It is very difficult when I feel better a small portion of the day, but suddenly crash for the remainder. I am tempted to look at my relationship with God according to circumstances and through the lens of not believing He is trustworthy. That deception wants to steal from me every time

Jesus, I **Invite You In** to dispel the lies and the attached emotions that are overwhelming me today. They are skewing my vision and marring my focus!

As I **Invite You In**, You, in perfect Joy, speak Truth to me. You never tire, become impatient, or lesson Your endless love! Thank you that You've got this and You've got me! You are indeed trustworthy!

> 1 Thessalonians 5:24 - Faithful is He Who is calling you [to Himself] and utterly trustworthy, and He will also do it [fulfill His call by hallowing and keeping you].

147

Jesus in the Quandary

Must I remain in bondage for years not knowing for certain the state of my cancer? The scan says no cancer, but the tumors are still present...HMMMMM. Is that a promising report? The doctor and nurse practitioner seem exuberant! "Excellent report!" they say. They have an eagle view. I do not! They see much more from their perspective which includes the physiological arena about which I can hardly formulate a question.

What if I do not know for sure whether or not the cancer will return? Does that really change anything? It doesn't change anything about You, Jesus, because You are the same every day. Living via circumstances is what has disillusioned me so many days in the past couple of years. This serious illness has caused me to question so much.

I **Invite You In** today because I do not want to be bound by any chains that seek to ensnare me if I just examine overall healing. I believe, as I have experienced during this season, there is more in You that You want me to become intimately acquainted with.

As I **Invite You In**, You are faithful in assuring me that being healed or not being healed is not the way. You are The Way!

John 14:6 - Jesus said to him, "I am the Way...

148

JESUS IN THE QUANDARY

After being dragged down by trauma, circumstances, loss, etc., there is sweet relief when those circumstances change. I have pondered many things over the past few years. I wondered what it would be like if I were truly healed and here I am with promising medical reports. Why am I happy? Is it just the healing of my physical body, which certainly affects my emotions? Or, is it because I have found a new place of intimacy in Christ? What a question? A good one for me to answer!

I have found that what A B Simpson discovered is also my Enough – "At last He said to me - Oh so tenderly - "My child, just take Me, and let Me be in you the constant supply of all this, Myself." And when at last I got my eyes off my sanctification, and my experience of it, and just placed them on the Christ in me, I found, instead of an experience, the Christ larger than the moment's need, the Christ that had all that I should ever need who was given to me at once, and forever..."[1]

I continue to look to You, Jesus, because this healing could possibly take a turn at any time, but You will not! I **Invite You In**, my Straight, Narrow Way!

As I **Invite You In,** You speak to me and remind me of the path I should walk and Who lights that path!

Psalms 16:11 - You will show me the path of life; in Your presence is fullness of joy, at Your right hand there are pleasures forevermore.

Psalms 23:3 - He refreshes and restores my life (myself); He leads me in the paths of righteousness [uprightness and right standing with Him--not for my earning it, but] for His name's sake.

Psalms 119:105 - Your word is a lamp to my feet and a light to my path.

Proverbs 3:6 - In all your ways know, recognize, and acknowledge Him, and He will direct and make straight and plain your paths.

Isaiah 30:21 - And your ears will hear a word behind you, saying, This is the way; walk in it, when you turn to the right hand and when you turn to the left.

Romans 11:33 - Oh, the depth of the riches and wisdom and knowledge of God! How unfathomable (inscrutable, unsearchable) are His judgments (His decisions)! And how untraceable (mysterious, undiscoverable) are His ways (His methods, His paths)!

Hebrews 12:13 - And cut through and make firm and plain and smooth, straight paths for your feet [yes, make them safe and upright and happy paths that go in the right direction], so that the lame and halting [limbs] may not be put out of joint, but rather may be cured.

149

JESUS IN THE UNBELIEF

Chemo drugs are no longer coursing through my veins and I am choosing to continue to eat healthy and exercise. Now I can focus on what is good medicine for my mind! I am finding that whatever circumstance, feeling, grief, pain, trauma or disease I encounter, my mind must not move from the Father. I believe it has become very plain to me that He does not change. After all, how could He? His character, attributes and nature are unchangeable. If I move from a place of love and life because of circumstances, then I have chosen to believe a lie.

What is special about this clarity is You, Father, are willing to take me on Your lap and whisper Truth to me, no matter how many times I believe the same old lie and feel the same old feelings! I **Invite You In** to receive Truth from You while You hold me tight!

As I **Invite You In**, I see that Truth stands for all time because You are Truth!

> John 14:6 - Jesus said to him, I am the Way and the Truth...

> Psalms 89:2 - For I have said, Mercy and loving-kindness shall be built up forever; Your faithfulness will You establish in the very heavens [unchangeable and perpetual].

150

JESUS IN THE DOUBTS

Following a clean scan, there is some assurance that cancer is gone, although tumors remain. Along comes the nagging temptation to doubt. The pertinent question is, am I, in the weakness of my flesh, going to believe a nagging thought, whatever it may be, that brings doubt and fear? For anyone who has suffered long and hard, like my precious little Christ-sister who lost her full-term baby and is pregnant again, is her temptation the same? Is her nagging doubt manifested in the question, "Will it happen again?" I believe anyone can insert his or her situational question here. We must all return to the Rock.

Jesus, I **Invite You In** to keep me from slipping into the miry clay. I trust You to put me on the Rock—the Higher One!

As I **Invite You In**, You give me the choice to believe. It truly is a choice of my will. I place my feelings in Your hand for You to exchange them for what You want me to have. I choose You.

Psalms 61:2 - From the end of the earth I call to You when my heart is faint; Lead me to the rock that is higher than I.

151

JESUS IN THE DECEPTION

Does the enemy ever rest? Undoubtedly, no! I am living proof because he finds nooks and crannies into which he shoots arrows—lies—lies which are riddled with negative thoughts. If I agree with them on any level, I become a victim of fear. I must take captive any lie that allows him into the battlefield of my mind; that's my responsibility. Within every one of us there exists, on an emotional level, a lie about God. The birth of all lies began in the garden when Adam and Eve hid from God. I, too, hide from Him when I believe that He is anything but Love—unconditional love.

Lord, if I believe that You do not have anything but my best interests at heart, then I fellowship with lies and will wallow in self-pity, covetousness, lust, anger, rage and especially, fear. Name any vice and the father of that vice is the enemy who spews lies. I am constantly tempted to believe that You are not trustworthy when negative circumstances present themselves. My current circumstances certainly do not feel loving at all! This is when I must separate the Truth from lies. Jesus, I **Invite You In.** You complete me with all that You are. You are my shield of faith, my Trustworthy One, my Love. All You ask me to do today is believe You.

As I **Invite You In**, You intimately whisper Your love messages in my ear and remind me who is really shooting the lie arrows at me.

Ephesians 6:12 - For we are not wrestling with flesh and blood [contending only with physical opponents], but against the despotisms, against the powers, against [the master spirits who are] the world rulers of this present darkness, against the spirit forces of wickedness in the heavenly (supernatural) sphere.

Genesis 3:8 - And they heard the sound of the Lord God walking in the garden in the cool of the day, and Adam and his wife hid themselves from the presence of the Lord God among the trees of the garden.

Song of Solomon 2:4 - He brought me to the banqueting house, and his banner over me was love [for love waved as a protecting and comforting banner over my head when I was near him].

1 John 4:18 - There is no fear in love [dread does not exist], but full-grown (complete, perfect) love turns fear out of doors and expels every trace of terror! For fear brings with it the thought of punishment, and [so] he who is afraid has not reached the full maturity of love [is not yet grown into love's complete perfection].

Ephesians 6:16 - Lift up over all the [covering] shield of saving faith, upon which you can quench all the flaming missiles of the wicked [one].

152

JESUS IN THE BATTLE

This long illness, season of grief, suffering and now recovery, is an all-out battle. The enemy certainly knows when I am weak. For instance, when I am emotionally fragile, I am very susceptible to the enemy's manipulations. He, the accuser, flaunts my illness before me constantly claiming that Jesus has abandoned me. There have been moments when I have been too weak and utterly exhausted to even hold on. However, in those moments, regardless of the taunting, I know that Jesus is holding me tight. Even amidst my temper tantrums, He knows my heart and He never lets go. I love the writings of the author, Staci Eldredge, who states, "All authority on heaven and on earth has been given back to Him, where it rightly belongs and Jesus gave it to us!"[1]

As is true on any other difficult day, I am standing and believing in what You, Jesus, my Redeemer, have already done and are willing to do for me in this moment. I **Invite You In** to rescue this maiden. I do not want to succumb to my emotions and the present circumstances. My inner-being is victorious even in this all-out battle.

As I **Invite You In**, You come to me as my Knight in Shining Armor, my Rescuer.

> Daniel 6:27 - He is a savior and rescuer. He performs astonishing miracles in heaven and on earth. He saved Daniel from the power of the lions. (MSG)

153

Jesus in the Fear

Amidst all my pain and grief coupled with ongoing questions lathered in fear, fear that tends to adhere like suction cups, here You are – Light—Life-giving Light. How much brighter is Your Light than the darkness of grief and fear? My heart bursts with an example of Your Light: my youngest granddaughter has come to You, Christ. At a rally, she wanted to respond to the altar call. Her Mother questioned her and asked, "Haven't you already made a profession of faith in Jesus?" My grandgirl's proof-positive response was, "Not like this!" JOY! New Life! Isn't that what we all crave?

Jesus, for so many years, I knew You as the Way and Truth, but I did not know You as Life, a life dependent on You for everything, even the precious air that my fluid-filled lungs have struggled to breathe in. I believe that of all Your names, "Life" encompasses the sum of Your characteristics. You are present every moment to be what I need You to be. On these struggling, very difficult and dreadful days, knowing You as Life is all that keeps me going. Eyes off You allow too many deceptions and feelings to slither in. They seem to give permission to catapult me into a fear realm that is very hard to escape. Receive Life, believe Life, trust Life. I **Invite You In**. Today, afresh and anew, I receive the gift of Life!

As I **Invite You In**, You invite me to Love. Love brings Light and Life. It not only covers a multitude of sins, it is a constant banner of Your Presence over me.

1 John 1:5 - And this is the message [the message of promise] which we have heard from Him and now are reporting to you: God is Light, and there is no darkness in Him at all [no, not in any way].

John 3:16 - For God so greatly loved and dearly prized the world that He [even] gave up His only begotten (unique) Son, so that whoever believes in (trusts in, clings to, relies on) Him shall not perish (come to destruction, be lost) but have eternal (everlasting) life.

John 14:6 - ...I am the Way and the Truth and the Life...

1 John 4:18 - There is no fear in love; but perfect love casts out fear...

1 Peter 4:8 - Above all things have intense and unfailing love for one another, for love covers a multitude of sins [forgives and disregards the offenses of others].

Song of Solomon 2:4 - He brought me to the banqueting house, and his banner over me was love [for love waved as a protecting and comforting banner over my head when I was near him].

154

JESUS IN THE DOUBTS

Germaine Copland, author and prayer warrior, writes, "My mind will not wander out of the presence of God."[1] What a statement! On the most difficult of days [believe me, in the grief, illness, and suffering process, there are many], I am never out of the realm of Your Presence, Jesus. You have come to live in and through me and this is our union. Living in and through me is an incredible Truth made possible as a result of the finished work of the cross. You have even given me Your mind. So many of my thoughts are fleshly and a result of agreeing with the arrows shot by the enemy. They are certainly not Your thoughts. I need You on a day like today, a fog-brain day, to bring clarity. I yearn for You to throw out the thoughts that bring doubt and fear. What a seemingly constant battle! I **Invite You In** to Windex my spirit eye so I can discern where these dreadful thoughts are coming from.

As I **Invite You In**, You remind me that You have plenty to say about what I should be thinking. Your filter of Truth will distinguish who is saying what to me! Discernment is difficult sometimes. Therefore, whatever thought does not line up with Your Living Word must be rooted out!

> Philippians 4:8 - Fix your thoughts on what is true and honorable and right...pure and lovely and admirable...excellent and worthy of praise. (NLT)

155

JESUS IN THE IDOLS

I once read an article with an intriguing thesis and from memory I will attempt to capture the essence of the story. Can explanations be thought of as a substitute for trust? To answer that question, consider the following imaginary scenario: God visits biblical Job and explains all that is about to happen to him, from destruction, tragedy and suffering, to the double restoration of his family and possessions. Job reasons that since he is to receive a double portion after all his suffering, he can surely endure everything for his own sake, not God's. He experiences an inner debate and self emerges victorious. It appears that Job serves the idol of explanation by using his own reasoning to distort God's narrative.

The story continues to explain the true reality of Job's story. God was silent throughout the entire debate between Job and his friends for one reason – God wanted Job to trust Him, no matter what. The reality of these scriptures is that in contradiction to the imaginary story above, where Job serves the idol of explanation, God clearly puts to death this idol by calling Job to trust Him with absolutely no explanation.

Personally, I call it my idol of "why?" Don't get me wrong. I've asked God, "Why?" plenty of times lately, but I have arrived at this conclusion, this Truth: do I want an explanation or do I want to experience the God of the universe by putting my faith, blind as it is, in Himself? I have finally come to a place where I do not need an explanation to be satisfied!

I **Invite You In**, Jesus, not for an explanation, but I just need You and all that You are to me today.

As I **Invite You In** to my Job-ness, You come to me and assure me that I already have my double portion—You!

> Job 42:2 - I know that You can do all things, and that no thought or purpose of Yours can be restrained or thwarted.
>
> Job 42:5 - I had heard of You [only] by the hearing of the ear, but now my [spiritual] eye sees You.
>
> Isaiah 61:7 - Instead of your [former] shame you shall have a twofold recompense; instead of dishonor and reproach [your people] shall rejoice in their portion. Therefore in their land they shall possess double [what they had forfeited]; everlasting joy shall be theirs.
>
> Job 42:10 - And the Lord turned the captivity of Job and restored his fortunes, when he prayed for his friends; also the Lord gave Job twice as much as he had before.
>
> 2 Corinthians 5:7 - For we walk by faith [we regulate our lives and conduct ourselves by our conviction or belief respecting man's relationship to God and divine things, with trust and holy fervor; thus we walk] not by sight or appearance.

156

JESUS IN THE STRUGGLE

Unconditional love. That is what Jesus gives, unconditional love. I, on the other hand, put conditions on everything: His love, my love, etc. There is this internal standard from which I operate that cannot be from Him. It colors everything I do. Even my healing is subject to conditions according to self. Certainly, there are daily duties to accomplish, but this struggle deals with my inability to receive His unconditional love for me. It is even difficult to love myself enough to rest—that foreign four-letter word! Taking care of me has become quite a feat. All aspects—mental, emotional, and physical, seem to be a challenge. Spiritual nourishment, the most critical of my needs, suffers as well.

Taking this line of thought a step further, beyond the difficulty of receiving Your unconditional love for me, is this nagging voice telling me, "It is not enough. I need to be doing more." Ever-Present God, I never want to respond to that inner, fleshly standard of "do", especially now. It always makes me ask the wrong question, "What am I going to do?" I **Invite You In** to answer the questions, "What do You want to do? How much of it do You want to do through me?" It is extremely important to rest physically, but I am seeing that my mind wants to prepare for take-off like a rocket. I trust You to answer these questions out of Your Perfect Love for me. By receiving Your love for me, I am able, more and more, to love myself.

As I **Invite You In**, You assure me, Jesus, that You are always carrying me. You are the Lover of my Soul.

Isaiah 43:2 - When you pass through the waters, I will be with you, and through the rivers, they will not overwhelm you. When you walk through the fire, you will not be burned or scorched, nor will the flame kindle upon you.

Hebrews 4:10 - For he who has once entered [God's] rest also has ceased from [the weariness and pain] of human labors, just as God rested from those labors peculiarly His own.

Hebrews 4:15-16 - For we do not have a High Priest Who is unable to understand and sympathize and have a shared feeling with our weaknesses and infirmities and liability to the assaults of temptation, but One Who has been tempted in every respect as we are, yet without sinning. Let us then fearlessly and confidently and boldly draw near to the throne of grace (the throne of God's unmerited favor), that we may receive mercy [for our failures] and find grace to help in good time for every need [appropriate help and well-timed help, coming just when we need it].

157

JESUS IN THE FEAR

From an eternal perspective, every believer can claim that they want to go Home and be in Heaven. But when faced with the reality of it, the view changes. The fear of leaving the known for the unknown is overwhelming. More than facing the unknown is the dreadful feeling of leaving those whom we love.

At this moment, in this concrete reality, Jesus, You have chosen to let me walk by sight in the promises You made for my healing. You have not asked me to leave behind those I love. I **Invite You In** so that I can fully enjoy this magnificent gift. Thank you for healing me as I move out of such a deep state of grief.

As I **Invite You In,** I give thanks for this excerpt from a Germaine Copeland prayer.

> Father, I believe that You have heard my groaning, my cries. I will live to see Your promises of deliverance fulfilled in my life. You have not forgotten one word of Your promise; You are a Covenant-Keeper...Father, what You have promised, I will go and possess, in the name of Jesus. I am willing to take the chance, to take the risk, to get back into the good fight of faith. It is with patient endurance and steady and active persistence that I run the race, the appointed course that is set before me. I rebuke the spirit of fear, for I am established in righteousness. Oppression and destruction shall not come near me. Behold, they may gather

together and stir up strife, but it is not from You, Father. Whoever stirs up strife against me shall fall and surrender to me. I am more than a conqueror through Him Who loves me.[1]

Psalms 56:8 – You have taken account of my wanderings; Put my tears in Your bottle. Are they not recorded in Your book?

Psalms 56:13 – For You have rescued my soul from death, Yes, and my feet from stumbling, so that I may walk before God in the light of life.

Job 14:5 - Since a man's days are already determined, and the number of his months is wholly in Your control, and he cannot pass the bounds of his allotted time—

Psalms 139:16 - Your eyes saw my unformed substance, and in Your book all the days [of my life] were written before ever they took shape, when as yet there was none of them.

158

JESUS IN THE PLAN

The author, Ann Voskamp, explains, "The literal translation of 'to provide' means 'to see'. God always sees—and He will always see to it."[1] That Truth can be a foreign concept to a "doer" like me. I inhale deeply with a great sense of relief as I read these words. Already, with a little bit of feel-good going on, I am planning in my mind what the next days, months must look like. Time with family, satisfying work, maybe a little fun, also foreign to the "doers", all top the list of what I am looking forward to!

My boss has always encouraged our staff with this explanation: God is not a teaching God, that is not one of His names, but He is a God that draws us into intimacy with Himself. I now understand that provision lies in that intimacy! Maybe I have learned something the last few years!

I **Invite You In**, most intimate God.

As I **Invite You In**, You gladly reveal to me that You are the Living, Loving God Who will see to my every need.

> Proverbs 16:9 - A man's mind plans his way, but the Lord directs his steps and makes them sure.

> Philippians 4:19 - And my God will liberally supply (fill to the full) your every need according to His riches in glory in Christ Jesus.

159

JESUS IN THE WEAKNESS

"Unto you, O Lord do I lift up my soul." Why do I lift my soul to You moment by moment? My soul needs refining! As I give my mind, my will and emotions to You, O Lord, I acknowledge that it is You Who will bring any areas of flesh (my way of doing what I want, when and how I want) into alignment with my spirit which is One with You, Jesus. I will then be able to stop trying to figure out what, when and how to live my life, especially the next steps in this journey. You are not going to judge my sin, Lord. You did that 2000 years ago on the cross. It seems that I have so many selfish, fleshly moments in my weakness these days. I'm finding that You simply want me to live free in the work You accomplished on the cross for me—which is LIFE, Your LIFE, free of condemnation! How wonderful! It's simple, but not easy, right, Lord? The simple part is that You are there waiting to live Your life through me. The "not easy" part is for me to surrender why, when, how and what's next! When will I open my heart fully and freely to Your love? I give all that concerns me to Your loving care. I don't mean to be in a tussle with You for control. It feels like that sometime—flesh vs Spirit. I really want what You want. I **Invite You In to** quieten my soul. That is where I find healing.

As I **Invite You In**, Your still small voice ministers to and nurtures my heart.

Psalms 25:1 - To You, O LORD, I lift up my soul.

Romans 8:1 - THEREFORE, [there is] now no condemnation (no adjudging guilty of wrong) for those who are in Christ Jesus, who live [and] walk not after the dictates of the flesh, but after the dictates of the Spirit.

1 Kings 19:11-12 - And He said, Go out and stand on the mount before the Lord. And behold, the Lord passed by, and a great and strong wind rent the mountains and broke in pieces the rocks before the Lord, but the Lord was not in the wind; and after the wind an earthquake, but the Lord was not in the earthquake; And after the earthquake a fire, but the Lord was not in the fire; and after the fire [a sound of gentle stillness and] a still, small voice.

Psalms 23:2-3 - He makes me lie down in [fresh, tender] green pastures; He leads me beside the still and restful waters. He refreshes and restores my soul (life); He leads me in the paths of righteousness for His name's sake.

Psalms 138:8 - The Lord will perfect that which concerns me... (NKJV)

160

JESUS IN THE UNCERTAINTY

It has been another very unsettling day. With a great sense of urgency my thoughts land on one of my favorite verses, "Peace I leave with you; My [own] peace I now give and bequeath to you. Not as the world gives do I give to you. Do not let your hearts be troubled, neither let them be afraid. [Stop allowing yourselves to be agitated and disturbed; and do not permit yourselves to be fearful and intimidated and cowardly and unsettled.]" (John 14:27)

How is this continually possible, Lord? Peace is not something I must seek. It is within me—encompassed in the Life of Christ. You are the Prince of Peace, Jesus. The finished work of the cross has made that possible! This is all a part of the great mystery of "Christ in you, the Hope of glory!" You're not going to just bring me peace. You ARE Peace and You are willing to live Your Life through me and manifest Your Peace in every situation, the kind that surpasses all comprehension. I can see a peaceful place in my mind's eye. My peace is not in a place. That's just where I go to commune with You, the ONE who is Peace! There I ask You, Lord Jesus, What do You think about this situation, relationship, circumstance? How do You want to handle this? What do You want to do and say through me? In that place of communion, there is rest that whatever You want will be accomplished by my yielding to Your will and way (what to do and say) in the situation, relationship or circumstance. There, I can rest in

Your Peace. It is like no other! I **Invite You In,** Prince of Peace.

As I **Invite You In** on this very unsettling day, I am assured there is only one thing that can be between You and me that would keep me from trusting You—unbelief. The root of my unsettling day is the lie that You are untrustworthy, Lord, on an emotional level. This is deception! I am willing to set my mind on You and I know my will and emotions will follow.

> Isaiah 9:6 - For to us a Child is born, to us a Son is given; and the government shall be upon His shoulder, and His name shall be called Wonderful Counselor, Mighty God, Everlasting Father [of Eternity], Prince of Peace.

> Philippians 4:7 - And God's peace [shall be yours, that tranquil state of a soul assured of its salvation through Christ, and so fearing nothing from God and being content with its earthly lot of whatever sort that is, that peace] which transcends all understanding shall garrison and mount guard over your hearts and minds in Christ Jesus.

> Romans 5:1 - THEREFORE, SINCE we are justified (acquitted, declared righteous, and given a right standing with God) through faith, let us [grasp the fact that we] have [the peace of reconciliation to hold and to enjoy] peace with God through our Lord Jesus Christ (the Messiah, the Anointed One).

161

JESUS IN THE PURPOSE

When miserable days come along, days where I feel physically or emotionally ill, I believe there is no purpose to my life. Explanation? Inward eyeballs- my eyes are focused only on self.

I **Invite You In,** Jesus, to speak to me about purpose—my purpose. How about today when, grateful as I am to be alive, I cannot see purpose or good? I must have You define purpose for me. I cannot seem to wrap my mind and emotions around it.

As I **Invite You In,** I return to reality that purpose is not something I have to define. It is not centered on my "doing" anything. It's accomplished as I rest in You, Lord.

> Psalms 57:2 - I will cry to God Most High, Who performs on my behalf and rewards me [Who brings to pass His purposes for me and surely completes them]!

> James 5:11 - We count those blessed who endured. You have heard of the endurance of Job and have seen the outcome of the Lord's dealings that the Lord is full of compassion and is merciful.

> Exodus 9:16 - But for this very purpose have I let you live, that I might show you My power, and that My name may be declared throughout all the earth.

162

JESUS IN THE LOSS

Ann Voskamp encourages us with these words, "Every little thing is going to be okay because God is working through every little thing."[1] The big trauma of illness and loss that has often defeated me is comprised of so many "little things" which encompass the details of life. Are You in every detail, Lord? I know that You are in the center of the particulars of my life: in the tears, the fight (grief sufferers know this well!), the pit, and the dark. I know that as **I Invite You In** to those places, You are the only One Who knows and cares about every detail of my life to the Nth degree.

As I **Invite You In**, You gather me in Your arms, Jesus, just for love and assurance. This is really what I need: a Father, a Husband, a Lover of my soul to take care of me and all the details of life.

> Psalms 56:8 -You number and record my wanderings; put my tears into Your bottle--are they not in Your book?

> Psalms 116:8 - For You have delivered my life from death, my eyes from tears, and my feet from stumbling and falling.

> Psalms 126:5 - They who sow in tears shall reap in joy and singing. (AMPC)

163

Jesus in the Questions

LISTEN
I'm listening Lord. What is my plight?
A voice in the wind, earthquake, fire of night?
I look for the answers; I never thought it a choice
To come away, be still and listen for Your voice.

The Peace, the Strength, the Love it brings
Along the Way, it clearly rings
To commune with You day and night
The Truth—the Voice of power and might
RHB

I **Invite You In** so Your words can echo in my mind.
As I **Invite You In**, You are there to minister Life to this
tired soul.

> Psalms 46:10a - Let be and be still, and know (recognize and understand) that I am God.

> Romans 8:11 - But if the Spirit of Him who raised Jesus from the dead dwells in you, He who raised Christ Jesus from the dead will also give life to your mortal bodies through His Spirit who dwells in you.

164

JESUS IN THE PURPOSE

My friend and co-minister at Journey In Christ, Gregg Gibbons, has suffered tremendously. He writes from experience when he beautifully expresses the Truth he has harvested when he states, "We don't produce good works for Christ, we walk with Christ in them."[1] I must say, this illness does not feel like a "good work" and I wonder if I am capable of this walk with Christ. I return to Psalm 41:4; and, so as not to measure His Love or my worth by circumstances, I must see that the greater work here is inner healing. In order to experience that healing, I must walk with Jesus. Otherwise, I will follow the lies that my feelings are attached to!

Lord, I know from the study of the Truths of the New Covenant that the work of completion in Christ is accomplished. It was done so at the cross. My soul (mind, will and emotions), however, does not always recognize healing and, most importantly, believe the Truth every day. I conclude that when days like today come along and physical exhaustion and emotional longing grab hold, You call me to Yourself and Your desire is for me to trust You as my Enough. Amazing! That's a good work You are calling me to. I gladly receive it! Trusting You certainly transcends these rough and tough moments! I **Invite You In.** I long to walk in this good work with You. No! I choose to walk in this good work with You.

As I **Invite You In,** I desire to respond out of Your Life to be one who is more pliable in Your hands. I know that my willingness not to react out of my flesh, but to walk in Truth, the Spirit, is my healing. You work Your way in me, regardless of circumstances and feelings.

Ephesians 3:16 - that He would grant you, according to the riches of His glory, to be strengthened with power through His Spirit in the inner man,.

Psalms 23:2-3 - He makes me lie down in green pastures; He leads me beside quiet waters. He restores my soul; He guides me in the paths of righteousness For His name's sake.

Ephesians 2:10 - For we are God's [own] handiwork (His workmanship), recreated in Christ Jesus, [born anew] that we may do those good works which God predestined (planned beforehand) for us [taking paths which He prepared ahead of time], that we should walk in them [living the good life which He prearranged and made ready for us to live].

Philippians 1:6 - And I am convinced and sure of this very thing, that He Who began a good work in you will continue until the day of Jesus Christ [right up to the time of His return], developing [that good work] and perfecting and bringing it to full completion in you.

Isaiah 64:8 - Yet, O Lord, You are our Father; we are the clay, and You our Potter, and we all are the work of Your hand.

165

JESUS IN THE DOUBTS

I am discovering that this part of the healing journey is very difficult in a new way. My mind travels to places that my body and emotions cannot. That sounds like a complaint and as one who often gets her needs met through performance, I guess it is. I want so badly to get out and get back to my "normal" routine, filled with good energy, mental alertness and emotional wherewithal. But I am not there yet!

Lord, I really do not want to miss anything here. I seem to be overlooking the moment and, certainly, I am jumping ahead of it. I return to the question that I know You want asked! What do You want during this time, Jesus? You seem to answer in a poem…

I, a doubting Thomas, how could I miss it was You?
Out there in the world, oh there's much for me to do.
I come to Your feet; You only want my time
I hear, "Come away with me, You are mine"

I've worked so hard; I am tethered and tired
Green pastures You offer; I can come up from the mire
How could I have doubted? Oh I had it wrong!
All along You were wooing singing me a love song

"Come to me and rest; come and lay it all down
It's in Me, not the world that all needed is found
So, I can come freely? Nothing for me to "do"?

I had looked for things When all along it was You,
Jesus!
RHB

I **Invite You In** so that I can rest in You.

As I **Invite You In**, I see the invitation has always been by Your Spirit and The Living Word.

> 2 Corinthians 12:9-10 - But He said to me, My grace (My favor and loving-kindness and mercy) is enough for you [sufficient against any danger and enables you to bear the trouble manfully]; for My strength and power are made perfect (fulfilled and completed) and show themselves most effective in [your] weakness. Therefore, I will all the more gladly glory in my weaknesses and infirmities, that the strength and power of Christ (the Messiah) may rest (yes, may pitch a tent over and dwell) upon me! So for the sake of Christ, I am well pleased and take pleasure in infirmities, insults, hardships, persecutions, perplexities and distresses; for when I am weak [in human strength], then am I [truly] strong (able, powerful in divine strength).

> Matthew 11:28 - Come to Me, all you who labor and are heavy-laden and overburdened, and I will cause you to rest. [I will ease and relieve and refresh your souls.]

166

JESUS IN THE QUESTIONS

Ann Voskamp wisely states, "Struggling and rejoicing are not two chronological steps one following the other, but two concurrent movements, one fluid with the other. As the cold can move you deeper toward the fire, struggling can move you deeper toward God, who warms you with joy. Struggling can deepen joy…The secret of joy is always a matter of focus: a resolute focusing on the Father, not on the fear."[1]

Jesus, do I believe that You are going to remove the cancer in my body (or whatever struggle that has led you, the reader, to this moment), and just abandon me and leave me here, discontent and joyless? I recognize that question as a new fear arising all because I cannot perceive or imagine the next step. After weeks of the same, low mental and physical energy, I'm ready to move on! Aren't You Lord? What's that You say? There is Joy in the journey, even contentment? Oh! I **Invite You In!** Please tell me more. More importantly, work that in me, Lord. I gladly receive!

As I **Invite You In**, You gladly take me to the Living, active Word to focus on what True Joy is!

> Psalms 5:11 - But let all those who take refuge and put their trust in You rejoice; let them ever sing and shout for joy, because You make a covering over them and defend them; let those also who love Your name be joyful in You and be in high spirits.

167

Jesus in the Grief

Author John Eldredge states, "The road to life and joy lies through, not around, the heart sickness of hope deferred."[1] I am taking a good look at this because I do not see anyone around me unscathed by grief resulting in some sort of heartache. If I focus on a change in circumstance and count on that to bring me hope, I'm afraid I will be disappointed and therefore hopeless much of the time. Change in circumstance does not equal hope.

I am beginning to receive the Truth that my Hope is You, Jesus, not some thing or some change that a circumstance is going to bring me. If I look at You as my Hope, then I can walk on through anything, whether "it" changes or not! There I will find the way to Life and Joy. I **Invite You In** Life-giving Hope of Glory.

As I **Invite You In**, I desire for You to continue to reveal Your Life being manifested as Hope - never changing Hope.

Colossians 1:27 - to whom God willed to make known what is the riches of the glory of this mystery among the Gentiles, which is Christ in you, the hope of glory.

1 Corinthians 15:19 - If we who are [abiding] in Christ have hope only in this life and that is all, then we are of all people most miserable and to be pitied.

168

JESUS IN THE DECEPTION

If anyone had informed me that healing was going to be as much of a roller coaster ride as being treated for cancer, I would not have believed it! Several high mental and physical energy days occur and then a day in the pit grabs hold and all my fears seem to rush right back in! Don't I know better? How can this catch me so off guard? How easily my eyes fall away from You, Lord. I allow my feelings to be bearers of Truth.

Now hold on a minute, maybe I am a little more "street smart". For these emotions to feel true, they must be connected to a deceptive thought. Lord, I **Invite You In** to not only reveal the lie that I have succumbed to, but please, please quickly bring it to Truth!

As I **Invite You In**, I come to You with the lie that You are untrustworthy which is like an arrow constantly shot at me by the enemy. I repent for believing the deception, yet again. I put up my shield of faith.! You assure me if I will turn to You, You are Truth. I choose to believe!

> Luke 7:23 - And blessed (happy— with life-joy and satisfaction in God's favor and salvation, apart from outward conditions—and to be envied) is he who takes no offense in Me and who is not hurt or resentful or annoyed or repelled or made to stumble [whatever may occur].

169

Jesus in the Timing

Jesus, I am pouring out my heart to You about _____
(fill in your own blank today). I hear Your still, small voice
say, "I will take care of You!" As I listen further, I hear, "I am
your Other, your significant Other. I am where you are!" I
really do know that those are universal Truths, but today I
claim them as my own because You are speaking to me, right
here, right now. My heart cry during this grief period is to be
more intimately acquainted with You; to seek You in every
step of this journey; to be free of _____, no matter how my feelings lie to me. "Thy Kingdom come; Thy will
be done." I yield to You to accomplish Your will through me
in Your Way, Your timing. I trust it will be perfect. I **Invite
You in.** I give this all to You.

As I **Invite You In** and give You this concern, I am assured of Your heart for me. You will do a mighty work to
accomplish Your will in me.

> Psalms 18:30 - As for God, His way is perfect! The
> word of the Lord is tested and tried; He is a shield to
> all those who take refuge and put their trust in Him.

> Psalms 138:8 - The Lord will perfect that which con-
> cerns me; Your mercy and loving-kindness, O Lord,
> endure forever—forsake not the works of Your own
> hands.

170

JESUS IN THE DOUBTS

Author Ann Voskamp asks a profound question, "Why do I
ever doubt that God hears and starts coming before you even
ask?"[1] I consider this because today is a difficult, do not feel
good at all, overwhelming grief day and I find myself asking
the question, "Where are You?"

Jesus, You answered that 2000 years ago at the cross. I
was crucified with You, Jesus, and my "old man" with its
sinful nature was crucified, dead and buried. I no longer am
bound to my Adamic nature. Having been raised into newness of Life, one with You with Your Nature, Attributes and
Characteristics, my spirit eye can see You more clearly and
my hearing has been opened to the voice of Your calling,
"Where are You?" You have come and any question that I
have, any need that begs for You, You are already here. However, when I struggle, my vision gets cloudy and I cannot
hear as well. I **Invite You In** to reveal Your Presence to me.

As I **Invite You In**, You gladly visit me on difficult days!
You ask me to believe that You are present even when emotions scream otherwise and thoughts want to go astray like
tiny, scattered beads emptied from a bottle.

> Genesis 3:9 - But the Lord God called to Adam and
> said to him, Where are you?

> Galatians 2:20 - I have been crucified with Christ [in
> Him I have shared His crucifixion]; it is no longer I

who live, but Christ (the Messiah) lives in me; and the life I now live in the body I live by faith in (by adherence to and reliance on and complete trust in) the Son of God, Who loved me and gave Himself up for me.

Romans 6:3-6 - Or do you not know that all of us who have been baptized into Christ Jesus have been baptized into His death? Therefore we have been buried with Him through baptism into death, so that as Christ was raised from the dead through the glory of the Father, so we too might walk in newness of life. For if we have become united with Him in the likeness of His death, certainly we shall also be in the likeness of His resurrection, knowing this, that our old self was crucified with Him, in order that our body of sin might be done away with, so that we would no longer be slaves to sin;

Psalms 88:9 - My eye grows dim because of sorrow and affliction. Lord, I have called daily on You; I have spread forth my hands to You.

Psalms 62:5-6 - My soul, wait only upon God and silently submit to Him; for my hope and expectation are from Him. He only is my Rock and my Salvation; He is my Defense and my Fortress, I shall not be moved.

171

JESUS IN THE WAIT

I have often contemplated a verse in the book of Joshua where he reveals to us, through the Holy Spirit, the origin of true success. The author states that victory is found by meditating on the Word day and night. I believe I've learned this through my "can't do a whole lot for myself or anyone else" time, because success does not equal doing!

Lord, my longing is to emerge from this extended grief walking in "true success". Worrying about what I "should, ought to, must" be doing is pure law and wears me to the bone. I know You have the perfect answer to perfect success! I **Invite You In** to reveal that to me.

As I **Invite You In,** I confess it is difficult to avoid running ahead of You in my own strength, or lack thereof!

> Joshua 1:8 - This book of the law shall not depart from your mouth, but you shall meditate on it day and night, so that you may be careful to do according to all that is written in it; for then you will make your way prosperous, and then you will have success.

> Philippians 4:6 - Be anxious for nothing, but in everything by prayer and supplication with thanksgiving let your requests be made known to God. (NASB)

172

JESUS IN THE TIMING

I have been in a rush since childhood. Thank you for giving me plenty of time to think about this, Lord! I have repeatedly moved from one thing to the other or done two or three things at a time. Because of my illness, I have the luxury of time to reflect on the question, "What is the rush?" It is fascinating to me that You are not bound by time. Is time something man invented? You are certainly aware of it, because You stopped it once! My constant sense of urgency and my iron-clad drive kept me from enjoying the moment countless times. There is this epiphany that I literally ran around like a chicken with its head cut off (UGH!). I did not rest, abide, relax in You. Now, because I'm ill, I cannot rush. I must choose resting, abiding and relaxing in You! Focus—it's about focusing on You in the moment. That sounds so simple, but it is not easy, Jesus. I **Invite You In** to stop this madness. I cannot engage much physically, so please stop the race of my soul—mind, will and emotions!

As I **Invite You In**, You bid me to come to You.

Ephesians 3:17 - May Christ through your faith [actually] dwell (settle down, **abide**, make His permanent home) in your hearts! May you be rooted deep in love and founded securely on love…

173

JESUS IN THE GRIEF

Grief and suffering can take the wind out of proverbial sails for a long, extended time. I neither desire nor am capable of being active these days. The healing trek is erratic and has its own life form. One day I feel empowered to take on the world again and another day, I'd like to crawl under the world! I know the covers would be easier!

I believe I have come to some understanding that given the choice of comprehending this part of the journey or choosing You, I will choose You, Jesus, no matter how forlorn and questioning I have been. The answers to the age-old question of "Why?" really do not bring much satisfaction. I'm just left with facts and no warm relationship with You. For today, I have some vision and some strength. I want to be wise in how to use these gifts. I **Invite You In.** I am ready to listen to how You want to spend the day!

As I **Invite You In**, You assure me of Your delight in guiding the way—The Way. I accept The Way might mean simply relaxing on the couch with You tonight. Got snacks?

> Psalms 32:8 - I [the Lord] will instruct you and teach you in the way you should go; I will counsel you with My eye upon you.
>
> Psalms 16:11 - You will show me the path of life; in Your presence is fullness of joy, at Your right hand there are pleasures forevermore.

174

JESUS IN THE WEAKNESS

Today is not a day of strength. I am physically spent after only a little activity. I suppose I'm comparing today with past outings where energy abounded! Physical exhaustion seems to equal emotional exhaustion these days. Yes, the nervous system must heal, as well, after a trauma. Most of my life has been spent performing and accomplishing. I suppose I equaled those two with acceptance, even acceptance in the sight of God. I believed the more I accomplished, the more acceptable I would be. That took residence in my psyche like some crazed formula for unconditional love.

The New Covenant of Grace tells me that I can rest, abide, and relax in You, Jesus, because the work is done. I am already loved, accepted, worthy and secure in You. Therefore, I can even trust the time it takes to heal and revel in small victories such as simply getting out of my chair. As my friend John said after I told him how many Hallmark movies I have been glued to, "Yep, there's healing in Hallmark movies, too!" Lord, I **Invite You In.**

As I **Invite You In**, with You, Christ, I will be ready to answer the call when You are ready to give it. For now, it's movie time! Can we have popcorn?

Romans 11:29 - for the gifts and the calling of God are irrevocable. (NASB)

175

JESUS IN THE WAIT

I believe as unproductive and ineffective as I feel these days, some of the most important moments of healing are occurring. I am learning that You really do not need me up and about on a consistent basis. It is simply Your desire for me to trust You and believe that You are working in me in this grief process while I am sitting still! That's the most important healing of all. Work—"doing", even ministry does not equal my acceptance and worth. I can take worrying about all that off the table. You really want me, Lord. Me. Not my antics of "do"! All of my self-centered thoughts of how I need to do this and do that for You can just fly out the window. I can really say, "NO!" to them. All I hunger to do is **Invite You In**. You reveal Your heart for me during this healing time.

As I **Invite You In**, Your faithful, tender mercies greet me.

> Lamentations 3:22-23 - The LORD'S lovingkindnesses indeed never cease, For His compassions never fail. They are new every morning; Great is Your faithfulness. (NASB)

> Psalms 42:5 - Why, my soul, are you downcast? Why so disturbed within me? Put your hope in God, for I will yet praise him, my Savior and my God. (NIV)

176

JESUS IN THE DISCONTENTMENT

Stamped in my heart that one desire
To know You, Jesus, trusting You are here
There in my spirit like a burning fire
Leaning in to hear You whisper in my ear
Come unto Me and you'll find rest
Sit at My table for you I have a place
It's really what you want—for you, the best
To sit and gaze and look into My face
RHB

I have choices as I sit in the same home, the same room, the same chair day after day. I can attend my own pity party, not a very pleasant gathering, or I can rest and abide in You, Jesus. The Apostle Paul was correct when he said he had to **learn** to be content. If I allow my thoughts to wander to what I believe would fulfill me, why is it that I am tempted to choose most things other than You? I am just being honest with You, Lord. Day after day as I fast on a noise-less, activity-less day, amidst temptation, I am drawn more and more to what You want to say to me. I am even discerning how You would like to spend the day with me. You enjoy long walks and HGTV, too! Thank you, Lord that You understand how difficult it is for me to lay down the "do" mentality that results in a myriad of activity and just rest and abide in You. You are always knocking at the door of my heart. You want me to **Invite You In**!

As I **Invite You In**, I find that You are the best companion ever! I want to spend time with You! HGTV's *Fixer Upper* is on!

> Matthew 11:28-29 - Come to Me, all you who labor and are heavy-laden and overburdened, and I will cause you to rest. [I will ease and relieve and refresh your souls.] Take My yoke upon you and learn of Me, for I am gentle (meek) and humble (lowly) in heart, and you will find rest (relief and ease and refreshment and recreation and blessed quiet) for your souls.

> Romans 8:5 - For those who are according to the flesh and are controlled by its unholy desires set their minds on and pursue those things which gratify the flesh, but those who are according to the Spirit and are controlled by the desires of the Spirit set their minds on and seek those things which gratify the [Holy] Spirit.

> Philippians 4:11 - Not that I am implying that I was in any personal want, for I have learned how to be content (satisfied to the point where I am not disturbed or disquieted) in whatever state I am.

> Revelation 3:20 - Behold, I stand at the door and knock; if anyone hears and listens to and heeds My voice and opens the door, I will come in to him and will eat with him, and he [will eat] with Me.

177

JESUS IN THE QUESTIONS

Throughout the last several years I have surfed waves of illness and grief that accompany suffering. I have received a deep revelation into what the prophet Job describes as his "spiritual eye". This is a deepened sense of the Presence of the Lord which comes with knowing that He loves me and desires to have a relationship with me. Unfortunately, I once thought this love was contingent upon how much I could perform for Him. How wrong could I be?! Abiding in quiet rest while sitting and waiting is where I found the Truth of His love and desire for me. I believed that performance for acceptance was always demanded. Consequently, I performed. Ultimately, I thought this was for Jesus. I discovered, in Truth, I was performing for acceptance from others. Who wants to reap the intense pain of unacceptance or disapproval? Shockingly, what was revealed was that my intense need for approval and acceptance was simply my inner cry for an answer to, "What about me?" Who am I? Am I acceptable if I don't perform?

By receiving Your unconditional love and acceptance of me, Jesus, I am now understanding the answer to the "What about me?" question. You gave Your life for me so You could live Your life through me. ME! You want to express Yourself through my personality and physical being. The Spirit of Christ, one with me. This is beyond belief! I **Invite You In.** I am abiding in You!

As I **Invite You In,** You open my eyes to see You more clearly. You are right here with me!

Job 42:5 - I had heard of You [only] by the hearing of the ear, but now my [spiritual] eye sees You.

John 15:9 - I have loved you, [just] as the Father has loved Me; abide in My love [continue in His love with Me].

Ephesians 3:17-19 - May Christ through your faith [actually] dwell (settle down, abide, make His permanent home) in your hearts! May you be rooted deep in love and founded securely on love, That you may have the power and be strong to apprehend and grasp with all the saints [God's devoted people, the experience of that love] what is the breadth and length and height and depth [of it]; [That you may really come] to know [practically, through experience for yourselves] the love of Christ, which far surpasses mere knowledge [without experience]; that you may be filled [through all your being] unto all the fullness of God [may have the richest measure of the divine Presence, and become a body wholly filled and flooded with God Himself]!

1 John 4:17 - In this [union and communion with Him] love is brought to completion and attains perfection with us, that we may have confidence for the day of judgment [with assurance and boldness to face Him], because as He is, so are we in this world.

178

JESUS IN THE GRIEF

Grief glasses. In the last several years, I had to choose whether to wear them or not. When I looked through them, all I saw was solitude, sickness, tears and suffering. I lost my usual—my normal. I've come to terms with this and release any remnant of grief and sorrow to Jesus. I cannot heal emotionally from the trauma unless I do. As scans shine clear of cancer and tumors, I joyfully remove these scales and choose to wear my "blessed in the land" glasses. My testimony is changing from experiencing the roller coaster of emotions to gratefulness. I have been honest about how difficult it has been day to day and what was needed to deal with deception and feelings that have a life of their own when unattended.

I choose to change my focus and partner with You, Jesus, as You reveal how this part of my journey fits into Your plan for my life. I do not deny the ultimate purpose is to make me and mold me into Your image. I want to experience that change in my daily life and I want others to benefit from it. I **Invite You In.** You are the only One Who can assure me that moment by moment You will continue to walk with me, Your Bride, in sickness and in health.

As I **Invite You In,** You whisper special words to my heart...

> With a whisper You created me
> All You wanted was for me just to be
> But I twisted and turned away from You

And found myself something to do

Away from Your love, away from the rest
Trusting in myself thinking I knew best
But You had a plan, it was a heavenly plan
It would involve a man—The Man

To come and bring me back to You
Nothing, nothing, nothing I can do
But rest in Your love, trust in Your grace
And abide once more, face to face
With You, Jesus
RHB
I **Invite You In.**

Romans 8:29 - For those whom He foreknew [of whom He was aware and loved beforehand], He also destined from the beginning [foreordaining them] to be molded into the image of His Son [and share inwardly His likeness], that He might become the firstborn among many brethren.

Psalms 41:2 - The LORD will protect him *(me)* and keep him *(me)*alive, And he *(I)* shall be called blessed upon the earth; And do not give him *(me)* over to the desire of his *(my)* enemies. *(parentheses, italics are mine)* (NASB)

Psalms 41:12-13 - As for me, You uphold me in my integrity, And You set me in Your presence forever. Blessed be the LORD, the God of Israel, From everlasting to everlasting. Amen and Amen. (NASB)

179

Jesus in the Quandary

I ask again, am I better or bitter? I question this as I continue to walk this long journey. There are currently no guarantees, just the end of one kind of treatment. I continue returning to my routine while caring for this mortal body. I have learned that healing can certainly take place on many levels. Bitterness, in my estimation, means I have believed the lies of the enemy and allowed him to flourish within my mind. What a beastly thought! Because the battlefield is in the mind, where has my focus landed? I can honestly say my focus is in a better place. However, I admit, there are lingering questions. Why allow such a desperate disease? Suffering, uprooting my life, a near death experience—what was the purpose? Really, did it take walking these tight ropes for me to learn something?

Jesus, I do not believe You are just a teaching God but an intimate God! What I've learned from this is Your Way is perfect for what You want to accomplish and that is intimacy with Your people in all walks of life. Why and how? Because You are perfect and You are the Way! In this world, there will be trials and tribulations. I have walked this part of my journey for such a time as this—to deliver a story to be told; shared with the hurting, suffering, and grieving. I invite anyone who reads this to ALWAYS **Invite You In**! It is the only way to survive what the flesh, the world or the devil might serve up. And, yes! I am better!

To the reader: When **you Invite Him In**, you will find Him faithful every day, tailored to your trial. He lives and moves and has His being in and through You. Trust me, it's an opportunity to see from His perspective what He's up to! Yes! **Invite Him In!**

Deuteronomy 32:4 - The Rock! His work is perfect, for all His ways are just; A God of faithfulness and without injustice, Righteous and upright is He. (NASB)

John 16:33 - I have told you these things, so that in Me you may have [perfect] peace and confidence. In the world you have tribulation and trials and distress and frustration; but be of good cheer [take courage; be confident, certain, undaunted]! For I have overcome the world. [I have deprived it of power to harm you and have conquered it for you.]. (NASB)

Acts 17:28a - For in Him we live and move and have our being…

Psalms 56:13 - For you have rescued me from death; you have kept my feet from slipping. So now I can walk in your presence, O God, in your life-giving light. (NLT)

180

Jesus in the Anticipation

Over the past several years, I believe I have felt every feeling in existence! My constant has been to process with You, Jesus, as I exchanged the lies I was tempted to believe and the feelings that came with them for what You wanted me to have in the moment. What a blessing to slowly, sometimes stubbornly, finally **Invite You In** to the seemingly impossible places and receive the gifts You wanted for me. Time and time again, I obeyed and there You were, Faithful One, always on time, always bearing gifts. You freely imparted Your Life, Love, Grace and Mercy to me. As I strengthen physically, emotionally and mentally, I know that You abide in me and desire for me to **Invite You In** in to whatever it is I am experiencing.

In a recent time of worship, I gave You all remnants of hurt, pain and untrustworthy feelings. I know how harmful they are and how they are tied to lies that would tempt me away from intimacy with You. If there is one thing I take ownership of, it is that Your Truth sets me free. Truth is You, Jesus, and You not only seized those emotions, but You whispered in my ear, "I am your **Fountain of Life**!" My spirit eye saw droplets from the spray of the fountain coming down on me.

I believe You have given me the next step, so to speak. You will continue to deeply reveal Yourself as my **Fountain of Life.** I am very excited about that revelation. I know You will give me plenty of things to write about and share with others. For now, I **Invite You In** to do just that!

As I **Invite You In,** I anticipate a shower of droplets yet to come!

> Psalms 13:5-6 - But I have trusted, leaned on, and been confident in Your mercy and loving-kindness; my heart shall rejoice and be in high spirits in Your salvation. I will sing to the Lord, because He has dealt bountifully with me.

> John 8:32 - And you will know the Truth, and the Truth will set you free.

> Psalms 36:9 - For with You is the fountain of life...

> Colossians 1:11-13 - [We pray] that you may be invigorated and strengthened with all power according to the might of His glory, [to exercise] every kind of endurance and patience (perseverance and forbearance) with joy, Giving thanks to the Father, Who has qualified and made us fit to share the portion which is the inheritance of the saints (God's holy people) in the Light. [The Father] has delivered and drawn us to Himself out of the control and the dominion of darkness and has transferred us into the kingdom of the Son of His love.

> Psalms 41:13 - Blessed be the Lord, the God of Israel, from everlasting and to everlasting [from this age to the next, and forever]! Amen and Amen (so be it).

EPILOGUE

Yes, I live! I live to tell my story and even the greater story of how my union with Christ, true Life, got me through the doldrums and shadow of death. To say we have a faithful God does not even begin to impart the intimacy that I experienced with the One True Living God, Jesus Christ. He is a God who will put up with whining, temper tantrums, disappointment, discouragement, despair, hopelessness and depression even when much of it is directed at Him. He understands the fears, no matter how irrational; the loneliness, no matter how unfounded. I have come to understand the Truth of Jesus' words on the cross, "It is finished!" through the foundation of the New Covenant Truth of Galatians 2:20. He "finished" me 2000 years ago but I had not come to grips with what that means, and now, I only have a glimpse. I am waiting for more! In His faithfulness, He has imparted to me in my soul (mind, will and emotions) what He's already done in my spirit. That is the embodiment of the New Covenant and that is the sanctification process. Translated that means in my darkest hours, which this book reveals, He came to me in a myriad of ways to impart Life to me in the moment. That manifested in the quietness of my thoughts, a meal coming through the door, a tense voice of a worried friend praying over the miles for me by phone, emails from all over the world that I am being prayed for, my family and healing team always coming through, the Truth of His Word comforting me, over and over. Most importantly, I experienced His Love, Grace and Mercy, personally and intimately. As I look back, there was not a despairing day that went by that He did not minister to me, even though it might not have felt like it. Psalm 41:4 states that Jesus would heal "my inner self." I testify that my mind has been renewed to Truth, my emotions have begun to heal and that my will has been tempered and directed to believe and trust, then act. Hallelujah! He fulfilled that ever present promise that I held onto, that He would keep me alive and I would be called blessed in the land (Psalm 41:2). Therefore, my testimony is that through His faithfulness, His intimate pursuit of me, I have experienced the Truth of Isaiah 43:2.

> When you pass through the waters, I will be with you, and through the rivers, they will not overwhelm you. When you walk through the fire, you will not be burned or scorched, nor will the flame kindle upon you.

I have chosen to walk on in this life to experience His Life in a daily, moment by moment trek by focusing on Isaiah 40:31.

> But those who wait for the Lord [who expect, look for, and hope in Him] shall change and renew their strength and power; they shall lift their wings and mount up [close to God] as eagles [mount up to the sun]; they shall run and not be weary, they shall walk and not faint or become tired.

Praise God, it is only the beginning!

An Invitation to Life

God is the giver and sustainer of life; therefore, He never meant for us to live life on our own. He designed us to have an intimate relationship with Himself. He made that possible through the crucifixion, death, burial and resurrection of Jesus Christ. He gave us Life through our union with Him. That is made possible for you if You believe in Jesus Christ. He is Eternal Life. Have you received Him? He is patiently waiting for You to confess that you can no longer live life without Him. **Invite Him In** to be Your True Life, Your Lord and Savior.

> Romans 10:9 - that if you confess with your mouth Jesus as Lord, and believe in your heart that God raised Him from the dead, you will be saved (NASB)

> John 6:29 - Jesus replied, This is the work (service) that God asks of you: that you believe in the One Whom He has sent [that you cleave to, trust, rely on, and have faith in His Messenger].

> Hebrews 12:2 - looking unto Jesus, the author and finisher of our faith…(NKJV)

> 1 John 5:20 - And we know that the Son of God has come, and he has given us understanding so that we can know the true God. And now we live in fellowship with the true God because we live in fellowship with his Son, Jesus Christ. He is the only true God, and he is eternal life. (NLT)

ABOUT THE AUTHOR

Renée H. Berry is presently working with Grace Life International as a consultant, liaison, counselor, teacher, trainer, and retreat and grace group leader. She is based in the Charlotte, NC office. As a trained musician, Renée served as a teacher, church music director, pianist and organist for many years. She came to Grace Life in 1999 as a student of the Advanced Discipleship Training (ADT) two years after the sudden death of her husband of 27 years. She needed counseling and the Truths of the New Covenant for her own healing. Shortly after she finished the ADT, God called her to come on staff at Grace Life International. (www.gracelifeinternational.com)

She was diagnosed with Hodgkin's Lymphoma in 2012 and had a near death experience. This enabled her to depend on Christ as her Life in a way she had not before. Her called mission is to lead people to live the New Covenant by passionately embracing the finished work of the cross—forgiveness and union with Christ—enabling us to totally depend on Him for life and godliness. (Galatians 2:20; 2 Peter 1:3)

Renée enjoys writing the Truths of the New Covenant and has launched a blog to do so. Please join her there at www.reneehberry.com.

Renée has two married children, five grandchildren and two great grandchildren. She lives in Blythewood, SC.

Endnotes

Invite Him In 7: Jesus in the Grief
1. Dickens, Charles. *A Tale of Two Cities.* (London: Chapman & Hall, 1859), 1.

Invite Him In 12: Jesus in the Doubts
1. Prince, Joseph. "Joseph Prince's Devotional." *Joseph Prince's Devotional.* https://www.bible.com/reading-plans/28-joseph-prince, September 27. (accessed October 14, 2017).

Invite Him In 14: Jesus in the Darkness
1. Young, Sarah. *Jesus Calling For Graduates.* Nashville: Thomas Nelson, 2016, 40.

Invite Him In 37: Jesus in the Plan
1. Voskamp, Ann. *One Thousand Gifts: A Dare to Live Fully Right Where You Are.* (S.l.: Zondervan, 2011), 99.

Invite Him In 39: Jesus in the Turmoil
1. Voskamp, Ann. *One Thousand Gifts: A Dare to Live Fully Right Where You Are.* (S.l.: Zondervan, 2011), 156.

Invite Him In 40: Jesus in the Darkness
1. Voskamp, Ann. *One Thousand Gifts: A Dare to Live Fully Right Where You Are.* (S.l.: Zondervan, 2011), 156.

In Him In 53: Jesus in the Battle
1. Voskamp, Ann. http://www.aholyexperience.com. November 27, 2013. (accessed October 14, 2017).

Invite Him In 62: Jesus in the Surrender
1. Voskamp, Ann. *One Thousand Gifts: A Dare to Live Fully Right Where You Are.* (S.l.: Zondervan, 2011), 76

Invite Him In 64: Jesus in the Darkness
1. Voskamp, Ann. *One Thousand Gifts: A Dare to Live Fully Right Where You Are.* (S.l.: Zondervan, 2011), 156.

Invite Him In 65: Jesus in the Fear
1. Voskamp, Ann. *One Thousand Gifts: A Dare to Live Fully Right Where You Are.* (S.l.: Zondervan, 2011).
2. Farley, Andrew. *Heaven Is Now: Awakening Your Five Spiritual Senses to the Wonders of Grace.* Baker Book House, 2014, 156.
3. Prince, Joseph. "Joseph Prince's Devotional." *Joseph Prince's Devotional.* https://www.bible.com/reading-plans/28-joseph-prince. (accessed October 14, 2017).

Invite Him In 68: Jesus in the Discouragement
1. "Gone with the Wind (Motion Picture: 1939) — Trailer." 1939.

Invite Him In 74: Jesus in the Uncertainty
1. Voskamp, Ann. *The Greatest Gift: Unwrapping the Full Love Story of Christmas.* Carol Stream, IL: Tyndale House Publishers, Inc., 2014, December 9.

Invite Him In 78: Jesus in the Purpose
1. Young, Sarah. *Jesus Calling: Enjoying Peace in His Presence.* Nashville: Thomas Nelson, 2016, January 19.

Invite Him In 80: Jesus in the Doubts
1. Young, Sarah. *Jesus Calling: Enjoying Peace in His Presence.* Nashville: Thomas Nelson, 2016.
2. Hillsong United: Empires, "Touch the Sky", 2015.

Invite Him In 81: Jesus in the Darkness
1. Hayford, Jack. "Rebuilding the Real You." *Praise In the Presence of God.* Https://www.bible.com/reading-plans/347-praise-in-the-presence-of-god#!. (accessed October 14, 2017).

Invite Him In 82: Jesus in the Timing
1. "Messages." North Point. http://northpoint.org/messages. (accessed September 27, 2017).

Invite Him In 85: Jesus in the Timing
1. Eldredge, Stasi. *Becoming Myself: Embracing Gods Dream of You*. Colorado Springs, CO: David C Cook, 2014, 23.

Invite Him In 86: Jesus in the Struggle
1. Spurgeon, Charles. "Morning and Evening." *Www.biblegateway.com/devotionals/morning-and-evening, September 1, 2012.* (accessed October 14, 2017).

Invite Him In 87: Jesus in the Grief
1. Gillam, Anabel. *Lifetime Guarantee.* Https://www.bible.com/reading-plans?category=devotional, *September 12.* (accessed October 14, 2017).

Invite Him In 88: Jesus in the Plan
1. Hayford, Jack. "Let God Do It His Way." *Praise in the Presence of God.* https://www.bible.com/reading-plans?category=devotional. September 11, 2013. (accessed October 14, 2017).

Invite Him In 89: Jesus in the Turmoil
1. Gillam, Anabel. Lifetime Guarantee Devotionals. https://www.bible.com/reading-plans?category=devotional September 12.(accessed October 14, 2017)

Invite Him In 97: Jesus in the Purpose
1. Prince, Joseph. "Joseph Prince's Devotional." *Joseph Prince's Devotional.* https://www.bible.com/reading-plans/28-joseph-prince, September 27. (accessed October 14, 2017).

Invite Him In 99: Jesus in the Doubts
1. *Call the Midwife*. BBC, ETV.

Invite Him In 100: Jesus in the Doubts
1. Prince, Joseph. "Joseph Prince's Devotional." *Joseph Prince's Devotional.* https://www.bible.com/reading-plans/28-joseph-prince, October 2. (accessed October 14, 2017).

Invite Him In 104: Jesus in the Deception
1. Arthur, Kay. *Lord, I want to know you: a devotional study of the names of God.* Colorado Springs, CO: WaterBrook Press, 2000

Invite Him In 105: Jesus in the Search
1.Voskamp, Ann. *The Greatest Gift: Unwrapping the Full Love Story of Christmas.* Carol Stream, IL: Tyndale House Publishers, Inc., 2014.

Invite Him In 107: Jesus in the Deception
1.Voskamp, Ann. "How to Find the Heroes in a Suffering World." The Broken Way: a Daring Path into the Abundant Life, Zondervan, 2016, pp. 226–226.

Invite Him In 110: Jesus in the Weariness
1.Young, Sarah. *Jesus Calling: Enjoying Peace in His Presence.* Nashville: Thomas Nelson, 2016, November 1.

Invite Him In 118: Jesus in the Doubts
1.Simpson, Albert Benjamin. *Himself.* https://www.biblebelievers.com/simpson-ab_himself.html. (accessed October 14, 2017).

Invite Him In 120: Jesus in the Battle
1. Eldredge, John, "Ransomed Heart." https://www.ransomedheart.com/daily-reading/recent, November 30, 2013. (accessed October 14, 2017).

Invite Him In 125: Jesus in the Discontentment
1. "Dictionary by Merriam-Webster: America's most-trusted online dictionary." Merriam-Webster. https://www.merriam-webster.com/. (accessed October 14, 2017).

Invite Him In 127: Jesus in the Battle
1. Voskamp, Ann. *The Greatest Gift: Unwrapping the Full Love Story of Christmas*. Carol Stream, IL: Tyndale House Publishers, Inc., 2014

Invite Him In 128: Jesus in the Darkness
1. www.bibletools.com
2. Voskamp, Ann. *One Thousand Gifts: A Dare to Live Fully Right Where You Are*. (S.l.: Zondervan, 2011), 156.

Invite Him In 131: Jesus in the Battle
1. Hayford, Jack. *Come...and Behold Him*. Doubleday Religious Publishing Group, Sep 1, 1995,113.

Invite Him In 132: Jesus in the Plan
1. Voskamp, Ann. *The Greatest Gift: Unwrapping the Full Love Story of Christmas*. Carol Stream, IL: Tyndale House Publishers, Inc., 2014

Invite Him In 137: Jesus in the Uncertainty
1. Hayford, Jack. "Sustained Through Suffering." *Power In the Presence of God.* Https://www.bible.com/reading-plans/347-praise-in-the-presence-of-god#!, December 22. (accessed October 14, 2017).

Invite Him In 138: Jesus in the Quandary
1. Simpson, Albert Benjamin. *Himself.* https://www.biblebelievers.com/simpson-ab_himself.html (accessed October 14, 2017).

Invite Him In 143: Jesus in the Search
1. Augustine, *Confessions*, I, 1.

Invite Him In 152: Jesus in the Battle
1. Eldredge, Stasi. *Becoming Myself: Embracing Gods Dream of You*. Colorado Springs, CO: David C Cook, 2014, 59.

Invite Him In 154: Jesus in the Doubts
1.Copeland, Germaine. *Prayers That Avail Much*, "Conquering the Thought Life". Tulsa, OK: Harrison House, 1996, 80.

Invite Him In 157: Jesus in the Fear
1. Copeland, Germaine. *Prayers That Avail Much.* "Overcoming Discouragement", Tulsa, OK: Harrison House, 1996, 99.

Invite Him In 158: Jesus in the Plan
1.Voskamp, Ann. *The Greatest Gift: Unwrapping the Full Love Story of Christmas.* Carol Stream, IL: Tyndale House Publishers, Inc., 2014

Invite Him In 162: Jesus in the Loss
1. Voskamp, Ann. *The Greatest Gift: Unwrapping the Full Love Story of Christmas.* Carol Stream, IL: Tyndale House Publishers, Inc., 2014

Invite Him In 164: Jesus in the Purpose
1. Gibbons, Gregg. "Rest Stop"." Journey in Christ, Inc. https://www.journeyinchrist.org/. (accessed October 14, 2017).

Invite Him In 166: Jesus in the Questions
1.Voskamp, Ann. *The Greatest Gift: Unwrapping the Full Love Story of Christmas.* Carol Stream, IL: Tyndale House Publishers, Inc., 2014

Invite Him In 167: Jesus in the Grief
1. Eldredge, John. "Ransomed Heart." http://www.bing.com/cr?IG=F96957530CF8407FBAB9ACC03B 02BBAB&CID=1C7D19E73E1D6283073A12ED3F1B63DB&rd= 1&h=eYfaazQzS3KlRSJtqu4mhMiAEIEB-4JA5pR5ixBuWkI&v=1&r=http%3a%2f%2fwww.ransomedheart.com%2f&p=DevEx,5062.1. November 30, 2013. (accessed November 30, 2013).

Invite Him In 170: Jesus in the Doubts
Voskamp, Ann. http://www.aholyexperience.com. October 27, 2013. (accessed October 14, 2017).

_____